I0895730

PRAISE FOR
FOR EVERYTHING THERE IS A SEASON

"Jack Scott's journey is remarkable: from a youthful defender of the one true church to a defender of religious diversity; from a boy raised in the deeply racist world of the 1930s and 1940s into a committed anti-racist; and from his small-town West Texas roots to become a two-time college president, a California assemblyman, a California senator, and finally, the chancellor of the largest community college system in the world. Jack's story is also significant for the light it sheds on the forces that transformed both the Churches of Christ and the American nation over the past sixty years. A remarkable book about a truly remarkable man!"

—**Richard T. Hughes**, author of *Myths America Lives By* and coauthor of *Reviving the Ancient Faith*, 3rd edition

"Dr. Jack Scott is one of the most interesting men I have ever met. His boundless energy, his positive outlook on the world, and his expansive professional experience make *For Everything There Is a Season* a must-read."

—**Royce Money**, president emeritus, Abilene Christian University

"Jack Scott went from West Texas through Connecticut to a distinguished career as a college administrator and state legislator in California. It is a story of the faith of a young man formed in Churches of Christ who never forgot his roots but who embraced the ecumenism with which the movement began. It is also the very human story of a man who dearly loved his wife of more than sixty years and the family they created through great joys and serious tragedy. This is the story of America, faith, and family through one truly exceptional life."

—**Gregory E. Sterling**, Rev. Henry L. Slack Dean and Lillian Claus Professor of New Testament, Yale Divinity School

FOR EVERYTHING THERE IS A SEASON

FOR EVERYTHING THERE IS A SEASON

A MEMOIR

JACK SCOTT

Abilene Christian University Press

FOR EVERYTHING THERE IS A SEASON
A Memoir

ACU PRESS

ISBN 978-1-68426-103-1
e-ISBN 978-1-68426-830-6

Printed in the United States of America

LIBRARY OF CONGRESS CATALOGING-IN-PUBLICATION DATA

Names: Scott, Jack, author.
Title: For everything there is a season : a memoir / Jack Scott.
Description: [Abilene, Texas] : ACU Press, [2024]
Identifiers: LCCN 2024001951 | ISBN 9781684261031 (paperback) | ISBN 9781684268306 (ebook)
Subjects: LCSH: Scott, Jack, 1933– | Legislators—California—Biography. | Politicians—California—Biography. | Christians—California—Biography. | College administrators—California—Biography. | California—Biography.
Classification: LCC F866.4.S386 A4 2024 | DDC 328.794/0924 [B]—dc23/eng/20240129
LC record available at https://lccn.loc.gov/2024001951

Cover design by Bruce Gore | Gore Studio Inc.
Interior text design by Scribe Inc.

For information contact:
Abilene Christian University Press
ACU Box 29138
Abilene, Texas 79699
1-877-816-4455
www.acupressbooks.com

24 25 26 27 28 29 / 7 6 5 4 3 2 1

Dedicated to Lacreta Isbell Scott (1934–2021)

My loving wife
My constant companion
My amazing partner

CONTENTS

INTRODUCTION

What prompts someone to write a memoir? In my case, there were several reasons.

First, I believe in the power of books. Over half a lifetime in education has taught me their value. I have always enjoyed and been particularly inspired by reading biographies. Even in early childhood, I recall my mother reading to me from Dr. Jesse Hurlbut's *Stories from the Bible.* I was excited as I heard the stories of biblical heroes such as Moses, David, and Paul. I later would often read and learn from biographies of political figures like John Adams, Ulysses Grant, Sonia Sotomayor, and Lyndon Johnson; religious leaders like Dietrich Bonhoeffer and Reinhold Niebuhr; and trailblazers like Jackie Robinson.

Second, I believe writing a memoir offers me an opportunity to reflect on my life. The wise philosopher Socrates observed, "Know thyself." Clearly, this is not easy. But I knew it would be both helpful and cathartic for me to trace my life from early childhood to old age.

I believe, however, not only that this memoir is an exercise for myself but also that it could be helpful for others to read. As I thought about an audience for this memoir, I naturally thought that my four children and eleven grandchildren would be interested in the story of my life. And many friends and acquaintances may also choose to turn these pages. Yet even those who don't know me may find this tale of joy, sorrow, adventure, setbacks, triumphs, love, political involvement, and educational leadership interesting.

One subject that interests most people is change, and change is a central theme in my life. There have been many external changes. A change in geography: beginning with my life in Texas, moving to the East Coast (New Haven, Connecticut), and finally settling on the West Coast, in Southern California. A change in career: minister, professor, college president, and state legislator as a California Assembly member and senator. Even my family changed: my safe, secure immediate family of seven was transformed into six survivors by an unthinkable act of violence late in my life. But the most significant changes in my life have been internal. The reader will notice in this memoir that my views on life and religion gradually, but substantially, changed.

The theme of change is reflected in the title of this memoir, *For Everything There Is a Season*. This is the opening line of the third chapter of Ecclesiastes. The biblical author then follows this statement with fourteen couplets. The first of these is "A time to be born, and a time to die" (Eccles. 3:2). I, too, have chosen to title the nine chapters of this work with couplets that are descriptive of the contents of each chapter.

I have strived to be honest in this autobiography. Reinhold Niebuhr, the noted theologian, resisted writing a memoir with this observation: "Memoirs tend to be narcissistic, pretentious, only fitfully honest." There is truth in that statement, for no one is objective about his or her life. Clearly, this memoir is written from my own standpoint. But I have chronicled some of my flaws and mistakes. For instance, at times I was too slow to recognize the sins of my culture. I just hope my humanity, warts and all, comes through in this writing.

Finally, I have tried to make this story not only factual but also interesting. I will leave it up to you, the reader, to determine if I have succeeded.

CHAPTER 1

A Time to Recall, A Time to Sow

(1897–1933)

Figure 1.1. Jack's mother, Ethelda Cravy Scott

Figure 1.2. Jack's father, Will Scott

The blood of our ancestors runs through our veins, their lives flowing into our own. Certainly, my grandparents and parents live in me, in my children, and in my grandchildren. I come from sturdy stock. Like many Americans, my ancestors worked hard to achieve the American dream. Their lives were marked by courage, persistence, and strong character. Because of my parents, I have been able to live a life of achievement, material security, and general happiness.

In 1893, Frederick Jackson Turner, a noted American historian, advanced the thesis that the frontier was central to the formation of the American character. My ancestors certainly illustrated this thesis. My pioneering roots have shaped my family for generations. In the eighteenth century, my earliest ancestors came to America from Scotland, Ireland, or England. In the nineteenth century, many of their descendants moved south to fertile lands on the frontier. Then my grandparents and great-grandparents made the westward migration to the farmlands of Texas.

My paternal great-grandfather, Williams Henry Scott, moved westward from Tennessee to Hunt County, East Texas, in the early 1840s. By this time, the nation was expanding across the continent as a result of the Louisiana Purchase. The United States was becoming one of the great nations of the world, fueled by its booming economy and expanding population. My great-grandfather was determined to be part of this growing success of the nation. When my great-grandfather moved there, Texas was the Republic of Texas, having gained its independence in battle, defeating Mexico in 1836. It was then admitted to the Union in 1845, becoming the largest state in area in the nation. In 1861, at the outbreak of the Civil War, Texas joined the Confederacy. This legacy influenced Texas culture for many generations to come, thus influencing my ancestors. My great-grandfather's oldest son, Abraham Moulton Scott, was killed in one of the early battles of the Civil War, fighting for the Confederacy.

Like most states at the time, the population of Texas was primarily rural. It was largely populated by immigrants from other southern states who were attracted by abundant land to plant their farms. My grandfather, Henry Goff Scott, was born in Hunt County, Texas, in 1856 and grew up on the family farm. He was destined to be a farmer, following in his father's footsteps. On July 4, 1880, at the age of twenty-four, he married a local young woman, Sarah Jane Lewis. Like his own father, my grandfather had the desire to move west. So he sought out less expensive and more abundant land in West Texas. He traveled on the Texas and Pacific Railroad, which had recently expanded to Sweetwater, to explore this possibility. He subsequently purchased several hundred acres of farming and ranching land in the Plum Creek community, about three miles southeast of Sweetwater. He then moved his wife and three daughters to this community in 1889.

My father, William Hopkins Scott, was born on July 4, 1897, in the family farmhouse. My father's birth was accompanied by great joy. It was his parents' seventeenth wedding anniversary. More importantly, he was the seventh child of the family but the first boy.

As was typical of farm families of this era, my father early engaged in farming chores. As he grew, he plowed the fields, harvested the crops, and tended the cattle and horses. He began his education at the Plum Creek School near his home. This was a typical rural school of this era, where all subjects and all grades were taught in one room by a single teacher. I remember my father wryly commenting that what he remembered most about the early grades was being called up to the teacher's desk occasionally to recite the ABCs.

At the age of ten, my father suffered a severe attack of abdominal pain. In this rural area, little medical help was available. My grandfather rode his horse as fast as he could into Sweetwater, desperate for help. In Sweetwater, he found a young doctor who was new in town. Based on my grandfather's description, the doctor correctly diagnosed an attack of appendicitis. Rupture, which was the immediate danger, would inevitably be fatal. Although this doctor had never done an appendectomy, he agreed to do his best. He quickly rode on horseback to the Scotts' home. The doctor placed my father on the kitchen table, put chloroform over his face as anesthesia, and successfully removed his appendix. This no doubt saved my father's life. It was the first appendectomy performed in Nolan County. Medical care in rural Texas was rudimentary at the time. It is startling to realize that without this doctor's heroic efforts, I would never have been born.

Eventually, the little one-room schoolhouse couldn't offer the education my father wanted. So in 1916, my father decided to go to Sweetwater High School for his last two years of high school. At first, he was teased for his country ways. But he quickly solved that problem. One of my father's classmates pushed him as he went down the stairs. At the bottom of the stairs, he simply flattened the bully with a right to the jaw. This brought a halt to the teasing.

My father was strong; his natural strength had developed because of hard work on the farm. The school soon noticed this and invited him to join the football team. Although he had seen only one previous game and had no experience playing football, he quickly adapted. He was a regular starter and became an outstanding football player during those two years. This skill would later open the door for him to attend college.

At first, there was no thought of college. After finishing high school, my father continued to live with his family and help his father on the farm. He also earned extra money by breaking horses for neighboring farmers and ranchers. This was the standard method for taming horses. One simply rode a horse until it stopped bucking. This process was repeated until the horse was tame enough to be saddled and ridden. Obviously, this was a dangerous and bone-jarring way to earn money, but my father escaped without serious injury.

My father's time on the farm was almost interrupted by a call to military service during World War I. He was drafted to report for duty on November 21, 1918.

Fortunately, however, the Armistice ended the war on November 11, thus negating my father's call to the armed services.

Figure 1.3. Will Scott, Most Popular Boy, poses for his college yearbook photo, 1922

In 1921, my father received a phone call that would eventually change his life. This call was from his younger brother, Crutcher, who was living in Abilene at the time. He encouraged my father to enroll in Abilene Christian College (ACC) to play football. ACC was connected to the Church of Christ; the Scott family were members of this church. This possibility appealed to my father, so he made the forty-mile journey to enroll in college. That fall, my father became a college man.

He excelled in football. He played during the 1921 and 1922 seasons and was elected captain in 1922. That year he was also elected as the most popular boy in the college. My father had never had his picture in the college yearbook because it cost money. At this time, college athletes were not given scholarships. They were given jobs to help them pay college expenses. But since my father came from a large farming family, money was in short supply. Luckily, his older sister Zotie came to the rescue. She sold a pig to enable her younger brother to have a full-page picture in the annual as the most popular boy.

My father's attendance at ACC had many benefits beyond his participation on the football team. His friendly personality made many friends. One notable lifetime friend was his roommate, Don Morris, who later became president of ACC (1940–69). Also in the fall of 1922, a beautiful young woman, Addie Hayes, arrived at the college. She and my father soon began to date, and a serious romantic relationship steadily grew through a two-year courtship. In addition to his social life, my father always commented on how the religious activities at the college (daily chapel, Bible classes, and church attendance) deepened his religious commitment. This commitment characterized the rest of his life.

My father's flourishing college career came to an unexpected halt on June 4, 1923, when my grandfather, Henry, died of diabetes at the age of sixty-seven. My father left college to help on the family farm. Eager to put his education to use, he also began teaching school during this period. The next year, on November 22, 1924, he married his college sweetheart, Addie. That same year, he ran for superintendent of schools for Nolan County. He had many attributes that made him a good candidate. He had a gregarious personality that made friends easily. Furthermore, the Scotts had many relatives; this was a natural base of support. He was elected to this position and subsequently reelected to complete three terms (1925–30).

In many ways, my father had lived something of a charmed life to that point. His hard work had been rewarded and recognized, he was surrounded by loving family and friends, and he held a respected position. In July 1927, however, tragedy struck, shattering my father's world. On July 13, 1927, a son, William Morris, was born to my father and Addie. Nine days later, Addie unexpectedly died of an afterbirth infection.

My father was devastated by Addie's death. Not only had he lost his beloved wife; he now had an infant son to raise alone. His sister Zotie, who was unmarried, once again stepped in to help my father. She took Morris into her home and became a surrogate mother to him. My father moved in with Aunt Zotie and my grandmother. He continued in his job as county superintendent while also helping to raise his son.

Three years later, in 1930, my father took a bold political step and decided to run for the Texas House of Representatives, representing Nolan, Fisher, and Mitchell Counties. He won a hard-fought election and began his legislative service in 1931. By this time, my father was dating my mother. They had met at the local Church of Christ, where they both were faithful members. Their romance culminated in their marriage on July 12, 1931.

So who was this woman who had stolen my father's heart? Her upbringing was remarkably similar to his. Newton Ethelda Cravy was born on December 4, 1897, near the East Texas town of Groesbeck. She was the last of eleven children. Both her parents, Jasper Newton Cravy and Mary Jones Cravy, were forty-five years old when she was born. Five of their eleven children had died during childhood; untreated diseases such as diphtheria, measles, and smallpox took a heavy toll on children in the nineteenth century. They were among the many who suffered tremendous grief and loss in that period.

Like the Scotts, the Cravy family was a pioneer farming family. Although originally living in East Texas for over twenty years, the impulse to move west seized my grandfather. Soon after my mother was born, he pulled up stakes and moved to a farm near the West Texas town of Leuders. Then a few years later, in 1906, he learned of the Homestead Act, which was offering free land in the territory of New Mexico. So he and his sons, Bill and P. E., took a trip to New Mexico to explore this possibility.

The Homestead Act, enacted in 1862, offered 160 acres of free federal land to anyone twenty-one years of age or older. However, the terms of the act required that the owner had to live on the land for five years, develop the land, and build a dwelling there. Over two hundred million acres of land were settled under the Homestead Act; it was key to the settlement of the American West. The exploratory visit by my grandfather and his two sons led to the bold decision to move to a parcel of land located seven miles west of Plainview, New Mexico. Since the Cravys had two children who were twenty-one or older, Gussie and Bill, they were entitled to another 320 acres of land to add to their father's original 160 acres.

My grandfather sold their land in Leuders, Texas; he also disposed of the belongings and livestock they were unable to take with them. They outfitted three covered wagons for the long journey, including food, tents, and treasured belongings. My mother, who was nine years old at the time, remembered the trip as exciting and enjoyable. They would normally have a campfire at night and eat food prepared around this fire. They had sideboards on the wagons that would accommodate mattresses for sleeping at night. Occasionally, they would hear the sounds of wild animals such as wolves or cougars, but they were never attacked. They would also stop along the way to visit with relatives and friends.

In the spring of 1907, they arrived at their newly acquired land. They soon began to dig and construct a dugout to supplement their tents. Later they would add a permanent adobe house. It was also necessary to dig a well and begin planting and cultivating crops on the land. My grandparents had arrived with high hopes. However, bad luck soon struck the family. Rustlers stole their cattle. Then my grandfather fell ill. He suffered from a lung disease, probably tuberculosis, and he finally died on Christmas Eve 1909. This meant the family was reduced to a widow, three older children in their twenties, and two young girls: my mother, twelve-year-old Ethelda, and Leata, aged fifteen. It was a very tough life of frontier living, consisting of farming, tending to livestock, and gardening for food to eat.

Old photos of the New Mexico homesteads in those years show an unforgiving landscape. There are few trees, only windswept, barren land with mud dugouts or hand-built houses of unpainted wood. The people sitting in front of their homes are like the land itself: stern, strong, proud, with homespun clothing and determined faces. Nothing about the life was easy. Food had to be grown, water had to be carried from wells the family dug themselves, and wood fires were the only protection from the sometimes bitter cold of winter. I have great admiration for my mother's family, who survived hardship and the earlier loss of many of their family.

Like my father, my mother and her older sister Leata attended school in a one-room schoolhouse located three miles from their home. My mother was always an excellent student, combining her native intelligence with a fierce determination to excel. It was at school that she gained a deep appreciation for the frontier teachers. She determined that she would one day become a teacher herself. At the age of sixteen, she learned of an opening for a teacher at a private school funded by parents near her home. She applied for the position and was hired.

The following summer, in 1914, my mother and grandmother traveled to Roswell, where my mother attended a state-supported normal school for teachers. This intensive training prepared one to pass the test for a permanent teaching certificate for the state of New Mexico. My mother studied hard and passed the test with high marks.

For the next four years, from the fall of 1914 through the spring of 1918, my mother taught in a series of one-room schools near her home. It was not an easy occupation. First, she would need to rent a room close to the school during the week, usually with a family. Often her room was separated from the rest of the house by only a sheet or a curtain. The toilet was in a small outhouse separate from the main house. The use of this outhouse could be very unpleasant, particularly in cold or rainy weather.

The school day would begin with my mother arriving early to prepare the room for the students. The room usually needed to be swept. If the weather was cold, she would need to start a fire. Her students ranged from first grade through high school. She would apply discipline when needed, although some of the students were close to her own age. She spent her weekday evenings preparing lessons for the next day.

After my mother completed her teaching duties during the week, she would return to the family home on weekends. She would leave on Friday afternoons on her horse, riding over roads whenever possible. When there was no road, she would simply ride over pastures. She would reverse the process on Sunday afternoons so she could be ready for her school assignment the next morning. I have always been awed by my mother's courage in riding so far every week for four years, unaccompanied, in sparsely populated rural New Mexico.

Finally, after four arduous years, my mother decided she did not want to spend the rest of her life teaching in one-room schools in rural New Mexico. Like my father, my mother was ambitious for more education, for greater opportunities. So in the fall of 1918, she moved to Fort Worth, Texas, to study bookkeeping at Draughon Business College. She and several other young women boarded at the YWCA dormitory. But 1918 was marked by the Spanish flu epidemic. This deadly virus killed 650,000 people in the United States and over 20 million worldwide. Mother received word that several of her family members in Plainview,

New Mexico, were sick with the flu. She cut short her studies and rushed home to help her family. Fortunately, all her family survived.

With her family safe, Mother decided to return to Texas and seek employment as a bookkeeper. Eventually, she settled in Sweetwater near the oldest Cravy sister, Florence, who had not moved to New Mexico with the rest of the family. She had married Lane Hardy in 1899, and she and her husband were the first in the family to move to Sweetwater.

Sweetwater was in sharp contrast to the barren landscape of eastern New Mexico. The pretty, tree-shaded streets of the thriving little town were lined with two- and three-story brick buildings. The dark red buildings with their white trim were charming. Parking places out front were filled with cars, though an occasional horse still joined the automobile traffic on Broadway, the main street. It is no wonder my mother fell in love with the town. One by one, the remainder of the Cravys moved to this growing community.

My mother was able to secure a position as a bookkeeper quite quickly. She was skilled, hardworking, and highly intelligent. After working at several bookkeeping positions, my mother was fortunate to be hired in 1920 by Levy Brothers, the largest department store in Sweetwater. The Levy store was a two-story brick building; it remains one of the historic landmarks in the town to this day. The Levys were one of the few Jewish families in Sweetwater. These brothers, Abe and Ike Levy, had emigrated from Russia, and their business acumen and hard work had led to their success. Like my own family, the Levys had started their lives in America as pioneers, selling goods from a covered wagon in West Texas. Abe Levy, the manager of the store, soon recognized my mother's ability and elevated her to office manager. My mother was not only a loyal employee; she became a friend and neighbor of the extended Levy family. Obviously, anti-Semitism was not a problem in our home.

Mother's successful business career enabled her to buy a house, a rare achievement for a woman in those days. She opened this home to her bachelor brother, Bill, and to her elderly mother. It pleased her to provide some of the nicer things to her mother, who had spent most of her life struggling to keep house on the frontier. And working in the store enabled Mother to dress nicely, since she had the first pick of the new fashions that came into the store.

Eventually, fate intervened in the person of Vanabelle Crossthwaite, a friend of my mother. Mrs. Crossthwaite invited my mother to come with her to the Church of Christ. My mother was attracted to this church; the fact that it strictly followed the teachings of the Bible particularly appealed to her. She was soon baptized, and she became a dedicated member of Churches of Christ until her death. The church brought her spiritual sustenance; it also brought her a new life when she met my father. My widower father found love a few years after his first wife's death.

My mother and father's marriage occurred on July 12, 1931, in the home of Batsell Baxter, president of ACC, my father's alma mater. My parents then traveled to Austin, since my father, a member of the Texas House of Representatives, had to attend a special session of the legislature. As was typical of that period, my mother chose to resign from her job after marriage. Upon their return to Sweetwater, my mother brought my father's son, four-year-old Morris, into their home. She became his mother from that time forward. Then two years later, on August 24, 1933, I was born in Sweetwater Hospital.

As I reflect on my parents' lives, it is clear how profoundly they influenced me. Clearly, their religious faith deeply impacted me. But there were many other traits in which they were my role models. My father was a gregarious, extroverted personality who genuinely loved people and made friends easily. I learned from him. I recall that when I left for college, he told me, "Jack, make friends of the janitor; you never know when you'll need a friend." His example was before me when I assumed leadership roles in education and politics later in life.

My mother's early experience as both a student and a teacher in one-room schools embedded in her a love for education that she passed on to me. She taught me at home in my preschool days. She saw to it that we had books in our home. I still recall perusing the *World Book Encyclopedia* that she purchased. She took careful notice of the report card I brought home from school. And she was very proud of my educational accomplishments, from elementary school through my PhD. It was therefore natural that my main career would be in education.

And the common patterns that shaped my parents' lives would also shape mine. Both had humble beginnings: life on the farm was not easy. But by hard work, persistence, and solid character, they were able to achieve remarkable success. I knew I would have to imitate those traits in order to succeed. Both my father and mother were persons of absolute integrity. Their word was their bond. As children, my siblings and I knew that our parents would not tolerate a failure to tell the truth. Most of all, my parents' relationship was the model for my own sixty-six-year marriage. They loved each other deeply and formed a beautiful marriage that lasted for fifty years, until my father's death in 1981. All this provided the loving, stable home into which I was born.

CHAPTER 2

A Time to Be Born, A Time to Grow

(1933–1950)

Figure 2.1. Jack's baby picture, age one

Figure 2.2. Jack and his sister, Patsy, ages seven and six, dressed up for a wedding shower, ca. 1939

At the time of my birth in 1933, Sweetwater was a dusty West Texas town of about ten thousand people. It was located on the main highway between Dallas and El Paso. It was a railroad town; both the Texas and Pacific Railroad and the Santa Fe Railroad were located there. Sweetwater was settled around 1877; it became the county seat of Nolan County in 1881. Agriculture was important in this semiarid region. Cotton farming and cattle ranching were the main agricultural enterprises.

In my youth, the center of the town was the county courthouse. The courthouse and the grounds took up an entire city block. Candidates for public office often chose this location to make their campaign speeches, standing on the portico of the front steps. The crowd would either sit on lawn chairs or stand on the lawn. Many other main businesses—department stores, drugstores, barbershops, and the bank—were located on the four streets that surrounded the courthouse. I spent many hours in these businesses in this central location: getting my haircut at Homer Long's Barber Shop, purchasing comic books at the corner drugstore, perusing books at the bookstore, or shopping at Woolworth's.

Since I spent my entire childhood in Sweetwater, the culture of this town deeply influenced me. It was my world, and I generally viewed it favorably. Within the overall structure of the Sweetwater culture, there were three subcultures that influenced me greatly: family, school, and church.

In many respects, I had an idyllic childhood. As I grew older and learned how dysfunctional many families are, I realized how fortunate I was. Although born in the Depression era, I did not live in poverty. However, I never considered my family rich; rather, I would classify us as middle class. We always had plenty of food, nice clothing, and a comfortable home to live in. Norman Rockwell could have painted my childhood.

When I was born, my father was in the Texas legislature, but I don't recall those days, since he left the legislature in 1934. My earliest memory was of his owning a tractor business. He first sold Oliver tractors, but when the Ford-Ferguson tractors were introduced in 1939, he switched to selling them. These small, powerful tractors were well suited for farming in our region. This, coupled with my father's natural selling skills, made his business quite successful. My mother was a skilled homemaker, keeping the house in excellent order, cooking nutritious meals, and carefully managing the household finances. She also used her bookkeeping skills to spend time overseeing the financial accounts at my father's business. We always had our evening meals together. This included my brother, Morris, six years older than me; my sister, Patsy, one year younger than me; myself; and my parents.

My first memories are in a house located on Pine Street. This was the house earlier purchased by my mother. I had my first haircut in this house. Lane Hardy, my uncle and a barber, placed me in a highchair in our kitchen. I recall a light bulb over my head. Since I viewed my uncle favorably, I submitted to the ordeal. A short time after that day, Lane died of a heart attack, and I recall the mournful gathering of relatives in our front room.

I was a healthy child who spent most of my time in play. However, one memory in that house is slightly different. One afternoon, Morris came home from school with the measles. Patsy and I were quickly infected. Mother placed us in bed in a darkened room because it was known that measles could damage the eyes. We all recovered; however, I remained convinced that the chocolate I had eaten the night before I got sick had caused my sickness. So I refused to eat chocolate for all my childhood years. Perhaps this illustrates a stubborn streak I continued to possess for the rest of my life. Unfortunately, the boy next door, Larry Loeb, was not as lucky as I was. He died of measles. Unaware of his death, I wandered over to the house next door and asked if Larry could come out and play with me. When I returned, my mother informed me that Larry had died. Larry's mother was the daughter of Abe Levy;

Mother had worked with her in the Levy store, and they had remained good friends.

When I was five, we moved to a large house in the southeast section of town. It was known as the Trammel House because of the original owners, who had built the house in the early twentieth century. This was to be our home from childhood to my time in college. It was a two-story house with four bedrooms, two bathrooms, a living room, a dining room, a kitchen, and an entrance parlor. It was located on several acres with a barn, chicken coop, and large field suitable for planting. This ample acreage was ideal for us children to play and explore: climbing trees, playing games such as croquet, putting up a basketball hoop, and staging rubber band fights at the barn. Morris had mechanical skills (skills I don't possess), and he could construct a cart or build a treehouse for our pleasure.

I was an adventurous boy, and sometimes I involved my younger sister in my risky exploits. When I was six, I led Patsy through an upstairs window for us to explore the roof of our two-story house. Luckily, it wasn't long before our neighbor, Nick Williams, spotted us and informed our aunt, who was babysitting us. My aunt, whom we called Auntie, oversaw us when Mother was doing bookkeeping for my father. Auntie and Nick rushed to us and told us to cautiously climb down a tree adjoining the roof, which we did. As we were descending, Patsy kept warning the neighbor, "Nick, don't you climb this tree!" Nick was very large, weighing over 250 pounds. Patsy was afraid that if he climbed the tree, he would break it before we completed our descent. When my mother returned home, she sternly warned me to never repeat this action. She told me that Patsy could have fallen off the roof and been badly injured. This shame was a much worse punishment to me than if she had given me a spanking.

My parents were very hospitable, and we often had friends and relatives over for meals and parties. The meal might consist of fried chicken or fried fish, some vegetables, watermelon, and homemade ice cream, prepared in a hand-cranked freezer. That was long before the advent of television, so we had to make our own fun. After supper, we often played dominoes. Cards were not allowed in our home because they were associated with gambling, but both sides of our family were avid domino players. "Forty-two" was the favorite domino game. The game would begin with each player bidding or passing. Then the high bidder would play out the hand to see if he or she succeeded or failed. This game was not restricted to parties. Often our family played in the evening. My mother and I would team up against my father and Patsy in intense competition.

Christmas, especially, was a time of much anticipation and excitement. The tree was well decorated, with gifts galore underneath. On one memorable Christmas, my parents decided to improve our musical education. I received a guitar; Morris, a mandolin; and Patsy, an accordion. Unfortunately, my guitar skills were not greatly improved by a year of lessons. Patsy, however, displayed real talent, becoming an accomplished accordion player, and Morris became a fairly competent mandolin player.

My childhood was also enriched by a large extended family, almost all of whom lived in Sweetwater. My mother's two sisters, Leata and Gussie (Auntie), lavished great attention on Patsy and me. Leata and her husband, Marshal Pior, were wealthy and lived on a ranch. When I was a boy, Leata would take me to their ranch to stay for a few days. She would often prepare special meals and spend time with me working on crossword puzzles. They would even saddle up an older gentle horse named Peanuts, which I might ride for several hours. I also spent hours playing with a cousin, Mary Ruth Cravy. She lived in a house a short distance away, since her father worked on the ranch. She and I would spend hours creating imaginary stories; naturally, we were the heroes of these stories as we fought it out with villains and soundly defeated them.

The other special aunt (Auntie) was fourteen years older than my mother and had no children. Sadly, many years before, Auntie had a stillborn child. The baby was overdue, and the difficulty of the birth caused the infant's death. Auntie was badly injured; no doubt the later practice of a cesarean section would have spared the baby's life and also prevented injury to Auntie. So we became Auntie's "children." We really had no grandparents; the only one alive at my birth was my father's mother, who died when I was five. Auntie was our surrogate grandmother. She frequently babysat us. If we were sick, she came to the house to nurse us.

Auntie's husband, Curwin, was the constable in the town. He was a large man, weighing over two hundred pounds. When I was at Curwin and Auntie's house, I recall seeing him remove his gun and blackjack. I was warned never to touch his gun, although he always unloaded it before entering the home. Since he was a law officer, he could get into football and baseball games for free. He would often take me with him, since I was always an avid sports fan. On one occasion, when my uncle and I were at a high school football game, I recall he had to arrest a drunken young man for fighting. The young man was placed in the back seat of the police car, while my uncle and I were in the front. He kept saying, "Please, Mr. Cook, don't take me to jail." My uncle kept driving without saying a word; he simply drove him to the city headquarters, booked him, and put him in jail.

After her husband died in 1954, Auntie eventually moved to live with my parents. So even in our later life, she was a familiar person in my parents' home. She was intensely interested in Patsy's children and my children when they came along, as she had been in us. For instance, she rode with my family to California in 1966 to help out with the birth of our son, Adam. This was before we had an air-conditioned car. Imagine an eighty-three-year-old woman traveling across New Mexico and Arizona in the summer with two adults and four children and no air conditioning! But this was Auntie; she was always available to Patsy and me if we needed help in our homes. Auntie passed away in 1979 at the age of ninety-five.

On my father's side, there were many more relatives than on my mother's side. His seven sisters all lived in Sweetwater and attended the same church we did. His only brother lived forty miles away in Abilene. I had twenty-two first cousins on the Scott side of our family, twenty-one of whom were older than me. Everyone knew the Scotts; it seemed we were related to half the town. When a local girl named Bonnie Bland informed her father that she intended to marry Harley Rogers, one of my cousins, her father gave her one word of advice: "Don't speak ill of anyone in this town, because Harley is kin to everybody in Sweetwater."

The highlight of the year for the extended Scott family was their annual reunion on July 4th. The reunion was held at the Plum Creek schoolhouse, the place where the original Scott family had been educated. It was no longer operating as a school, but the building and grounds had been preserved. About fifty to sixty people attended the reunion; this included the original brothers and sisters plus their children, their grandchildren, and the spouses of the family members. The few who had moved away always made a great effort to attend the annual get-together.

When the Scott clan gathered, they hugged and laughed and told many stories. We Scotts were not a quiet bunch. Since dominoes was their favorite game, the adults played throughout the day. At midmorning, a program would be presented by the children. Each child was expected to recite a poem, play a musical instrument, or sing a song. Some adults would join in with a quartet of selected hymns. But always the program would conclude with our singing "Old Susannah," which was Grandpa Scott's favorite song. Lunch was a huge display of food, since each woman had brought her favorite dish. In the afternoon, the single men played the married men in a baseball game. I recall as a young boy how I couldn't wait until I was old enough to play.

One reunion really stands out in my memory. During World War II, there were eight cousins on the Scott side of the family in the armed services. Some were in dangerous zones, flying bombing missions over enemy territory, for example. At this reunion, I recall fervent prayers for their safety and all of us joining in to write letters to them. Fortunately, none of them lost their lives in the war.

Overall, my family life was nurturing, giving me the self-confidence that is necessary for a healthy emotional life. And there was discipline as well as love: I clearly understood where the boundaries were. But by their example and teaching, my parents instilled in me a set of values that proved very helpful to me in negotiating life.

In the fall of 1940, I began my years in Sweetwater public schools. I enrolled in Philip Nolan Elementary School (better known as East Ward) at the age of seven. After one week in the first grade, I was promoted to the second grade. Why? My mother had spent many hours teaching me in my preschool years. I had picked up reading, probably as she read me Bible stories. I also was proficient in arithmetic. My mother recognized my interest in numbers, so she would give me simple math problems to solve in church. I guess she realized that a small boy could easily get bored during lengthy sermons. I became so good at math in my preschool years that Mr. Armor, a local druggist, would call me over in the presence of some adults and give me some simple arithmetic problems. When I succeeded, he would reward me with an ice-cream cone. Only in small-town America!

School days were generally enjoyable. I was curious enough to enjoy learning and did well in most subjects. (Art was an exception.) The teachers in our town were dedicated and quite capable. I recall some solid instruction from knowledgeable and hardworking women. For instance, I remember Mrs. Foster, who taught us phonics in the second grade. I believe that my spelling skills have been quite good because of this solid grounding in phonics.

Like most children, I particularly enjoyed recess. I liked sports and took part in games with much energy. There were lessons to be learned on the playground as well. Occasionally, fights broke out between boys. Sometimes these were hard to avoid. I learned early to avoid fights, if possible; however, I knew how to respond quickly when necessary. I might not win the struggle, but at least bullies realized that I was not an easy mark. My older brother also gave me a few tips on this rough-and-tumble aspect of childhood.

World War II was a prevailing part of the culture in these elementary school days. I was listening to the radio on December 7, 1941, when I heard that Pearl Harbor had been bombed by the Japanese. As an eight-year-old, I didn't even know where Pearl Harbor was. But things soon changed in my Texas town. We would march out of our classroom and surround the American flag to recite the Pledge of Allegiance. We were encouraged to buy defense stamps that would fill a stamp book that could grow to $18.75. This could then be traded for a $25 defense bond after ten years. Rationing of tires, gas, sugar, and other items also occurred during this time. Americans overwhelmingly supported the war effort. We were all overjoyed at the conclusion of the war in August 1945.

By this time, I was enrolled in Reagan Junior High School. There was only one junior high in Sweetwater, so all three elementary schools fed into this school. I made some new friends and continued my recreational activities. After school, I would often seek out neighbor boys to play baseball or touch football. I also got a tennis racket and learned to enjoy the game. This was important because I regularly played tennis and became skilled enough to make the tennis team in high school.

In my leisure time, I became a regular at the local public library. I particularly enjoyed adventure books, such as the Hardy Boys series. I also began to read Mark Twain, particularly those stories that featured Tom Sawyer and Huckleberry Finn. Of course, this was the heyday of comic books, and I read my share of those.

One amusing event at this time involved Morris. He loved cars, and in high school, he had purchased an old Model A Ford. Always seeking ways to earn money, he stripped this old car down and placed a huge wooden box on the frame, leaving the two front seats intact but without a top covering. His idea was to fill this box with minnows in water and sell them to fishermen for bait. One day, he volunteered to take Patsy and me to junior high. Morris and I were in the front seats; Patsy and her friend Barbara Akins were standing up in the large wooden box behind us. When we hit a bump in the road, the bolts holding the box were loosened. Suddenly, Morris and I were moving forward alone, and Patsy and her friend were left behind, bouncing in the fallen box on the road. Aside from a few small bruises, no one was hurt. Of course, it could have caused serious injury. Fortunately, it just became another story of our adventurous childhood.

In 1947, I entered my first of three years of high school. As is characteristic of most Texas towns, Sweetwater was football crazy. However, at five feet six and 140 pounds at that time, I was clearly not destined for football. Although my father had been an outstanding football player in high school and college, Dad did not push me to play football. Rather, he tactfully suggested that I go out for the debate team. At college, my father's roommate, Don Morris, had excelled at debate, and Dad realized that speaking skills could be important in my future. It turned out that I enjoyed debate very much.

My debate partner was James Kirby, who was the son of the local Methodist minister and later in life became the dean of the School of Theology at Southern Methodist University. In my senior year, James and I won the district and regional tournaments. Indeed, the speaking skills I learned in debate would serve me well in the future.

Another skill I was able to use effectively in these years was my arithmetic ability. In the spring, Texas had a series of academic contests labeled the Texas Interscholastic League. One contest was known as Number Sense. This contest involved one hundred arithmetic problems to be mentally solved by quickly writing down one's answers in a ten-minute period. After successfully scoring in district and regional contests, I won third place at the state tournament in my sophomore year. Then in my junior year, I won the district and regional contests and won first place in the state final. My father accompanied me to Austin for the state contest both years and was very proud of my accomplishment. It was a great bonding experience as Dad and I traveled to and from Austin in the car and spent a night together in a hotel.

In Sweetwater, one could get a driver's license at age fourteen if the county judge agreed. My father first taught me how to drive on tractors; after all, this was his business. So I passed the driving test, and the county judge gave me permission to drive. Looking back, I realize giving a license to a fourteen-year-old was clearly a mistake. Texas has subsequently changed that law. I sometimes did not use good judgment behind the wheel at that age. On one occasion, I received a ticket for a driving violation. Hoping to hide this fact from my parents, I planned to secretly pay the fine from my own resources. No such luck! The next day, my father came in and said, "Elsie Robinson told me that he saw you were stopped by the cops." This is one of the curses of living in a small town. Nothing is private.

On occasion, I could get my parents' pickup or car in the evening. I would gather up a few buddies and drive around to see where some action might be. One afternoon, I had the pickup. It was a day when a rare snow fell in Sweetwater. I talked to some friends, and we decided to gather some snowballs. I would drive, and they would stand up in the rear of the pickup and pelt friends and other bystanders with snowballs. Unfortunately, at one stop, I thought I heard them say "Go!" when actually they said "Whoa!" One of my friends, Dale McCreight, fell out of the pickup onto the pavement as I sped away. He seemed dazed, so I took him to his father, who owned a music store. Now I realize he probably suffered a concussion. But he showed up the next morning at school, so I suppose no permanent damage was done.

My teenage years brought on the onset of puberty, and like other boys, I became quite interested in girls. In my junior year, a pretty girl named Carol Swart sat next to me in chemistry class. I finally got enough courage to ask her for a date. Unfortunately, the fact that she was the daughter of a Pentecostal preacher did not please my parents. In the blush of first love, though, I was not easily deterred. The infatuation and romance proved short-lived, however, since her family moved away in the summer.

Luckily, I did not navigate my teenage years alone, for I had my brother and sister as companions. I admired Morris because his life was exciting. At six years older than me, he was 6′2″ and handsome. Self-confident and extroverted, he always had a lot of friends. But these traits often led him to push boundaries. For instance, on one occasion, he and his companions placed a cow in the high school over a weekend. You can imagine the resulting mess discovered when school opened on Monday morning. I can still recall some heated conversations between Morris and my parents as a result of his antics. In retrospect, I believe my brother would have been more comfortable in a non-puritanical family.

Morris was drafted after high school graduation in 1945. (The nation continued the draft even after World War II ended.) I remember when he came home on a furlough, looking dashing in his navy uniform. He was accompanied by a friend he had made, a young man from Brooklyn. I was fascinated by this young man of Italian descent. I had never met someone like him in my small Texas town. Morris was honorably discharged after one year of service; he then enrolled in Abilene Christian College (ACC). He was quite popular: he was elected as a cheerleader and selected as a member of a leading social club. Although not a great student, he was (not surprisingly) well known for his pranks.

Throughout these years, he had a romance with a younger, beautiful girl in our local church, Estelle Tansil. She was quite talented; she was a pianist and had a beautiful soprano voice. My mother always thought she was the ideal person for Morris. This romance moved forward, and they eventually eloped and were married in May 1948.

Morris later told me an interesting story about their return from their honeymoon. They had been to California, but the car broke down in New Mexico. He called our father, probably for cash. My father simply gave him this terse advice: "Son, I think it is time for you to get a job." Morris followed that advice and went to work in a furniture store in Carlsbad, New Mexico. Being entrepreneurial, he soon moved to Pecos, Texas, and started a small business called Bill's Bargain Furniture. Morris was always a great salesman and was willing to work hard, so his life in Pecos was financially successful. He and Estelle also began to build a family in 1949; they had three boys, each two years apart (Billy, Bobby, and Harry). I became an uncle at age fifteen.

My other sibling, Patsy, was one year younger than me, so we did many things together. As children, we often played games, climbed trees, and invented imaginary stories to act out. And, naturally, we went to school together, since we were only a grade apart. We occasionally quarreled over something, but there was never serious conflict. "Jack and Patsy" was a familiar refrain. I have several photographs in my home of us posing together in our childhood. One memorable photo is of us dressed up as a bride and groom, to be displayed at a wedding shower. I was wearing a rented tuxedo, and Patsy was wearing a child-sized wedding dress. When Patsy and I got to high school, we regularly exchanged information about our dating prospects. Patsy was extroverted, was quite popular, had close friends, and as a pretty young girl, had many dates in high school.

In my senior year, I was elected president of the student council, my first experience in leadership. I graduated from high school in May 1950. I was third in a graduation class of 115. I look back on my high school years fondly. I made some mistakes, and like all teenagers, I had moments of anxiety and insecurity. Yet I made some good friends, had a lot of fun, and learned some things along the way.

There was never any doubt about where I was going to college: ACC. This is the college that my father, my brother, and many of my cousins had attended. It was located only forty miles east of Sweetwater. It was the college in Texas affiliated with Churches of Christ, which had profoundly influenced me from my infancy. Looking back on my early life, it seems almost inevitable that I would become a member of the Church of Christ and dedicate my life at an early age to serving it.

My father was one of the six elders of the local Church of Christ. In our church governance, the elders were like a board of trustees, which oversaw the church. My mother was a Sunday schoolteacher. Our family attended every time the church doors were open: Sunday morning, Sunday evening, and Wednesday evening. I gained a great deal of biblical knowledge and spiritual teaching during those years. The doctrines and practices of Churches of Christ were instilled in me from my birth. This religious body had been founded in America in the early nineteenth century. Its fundamental premise was to restore Christianity as revealed in the New Testament. The church founders firmly believed that if a church only took the Bible and rejected creeds and traditions, this could lead to unity.

Of course, restoration movements were not new in the history of Christianity. The Protestant Reformation of the sixteenth century had broken with the Roman Catholic Church, believing Scriptures should be the sole guide for Christians. Therefore, the Reformation rejected Catholic practices such as the papacy, the celibacy of priests, and purgatory as being unscriptural and therefore sinful. Strictly following the Scriptures was also the driving belief that later led the Puritans to separate from the Church of England and settle in America.

This belief in the restoration of New Testament Christianity found fertile ground on the American frontier. Men such as Alexander Campbell and Barton Stone, both former Presbyterian ministers, had great success in preaching this message. Under the leadership of Campbell and Stone, this message eventually led to the creation of a new religious body known as the Disciples of Christ or Churches of Christ. According to the US Census of 1860, this church rapidly grew to 192,323 members and continued this solid growth throughout the nineteenth century.

But the restoration of New Testament Christianity has some inherent problems. It requires the interpretation of the Scriptures. Which doctrines and practices of the first century are essential, and which are merely part of the culture of that time—and therefore nonessential? For instance, most believers in strict restoration believe that the early church baptized adults by immersion rather than baptizing infants by sprinkling. Most biblical scholars would agree that this practice was true of the first-century church. So, many churches consider this form of baptism mandatory for Christians today. However, a vast majority of current churches consider Paul's commandment for women to cover their heads at worship (1 Cor. 11:2–10) as part of first-century culture and not mandatory for women in church today. Restoration churches rejected the notion of written creeds, but the unwritten doctrines resulting from scriptural interpretation created division and strife.

In the latter half of the nineteenth century, disagreements arose in the Stone-Campbell movement over what doctrines and practices were essential in the restoration of New Testament Christianity. The two most serious differences were over whether instrumental music could be used in worship and whether a church could support a missionary society. These differences became so serious that they eventually led to division.

Churches of Christ believed that these practices were unscriptural, but the Disciples of Christ did not believe they were. So in 1906, the US Census listed Churches of Christ and the Disciples of Christ as separate denominations. Actually, it was clear that this division had existed for some time. The Census merely formalized it.

Over time, Churches of Christ adopted an increasingly separatist view toward other churches. For instance, in Sweetwater and in most other Churches of Christ, our minister did not belong to the local ministerial alliance. We considered ourselves the "true church," and we labeled the other churches as the "denominations." They were the "other." I still recall attending my uncle John's funeral in the Methodist church. It felt strange to hear the organ play and see the stained glass windows, neither of which was allowed in Churches of Christ.

Other practices set Churches of Christ apart from the denominations. There was no choir in our church; we had congregational singing led by a song leader. No minister was referred to as "Father" or "Reverend." Members of the church called each other "Brother" or "Sister." Our churches had a baptistery at the front of the church. In this tank of water, persons were immersed publicly to become members of the church. The minister normally performed this ceremony. Both the minister and the person being baptized changed clothes prior to the baptism. I was baptized at the age of twelve. I had read in the New Testament that at age twelve, Jesus had said that "I must be about my Father's business" (Luke 2:49 KJV). So shortly after I turned twelve, I announced to my parents that I wanted to be baptized. I can clearly recall that Sunday and how seriously I took that commitment.

In my church, I was taught a strict moral code. Activities such as the drinking of alcoholic beverages, gambling, and dancing were viewed as sinful. Dancing was prohibited because it could incite sexual desire and lead to prohibited behavior. Divorce was forbidden except in the case of adultery. Although I was taught this rather strict code of behavior, my parents also practiced and taught central themes of the gospel such as absolute honesty, love of neighbor, kindness, and other virtues. Religion was central in our home. My parents took their Christianity very seriously. So by their teaching and example, I was taught a set of values that proved very helpful to me in life.

These values also influenced my choice of career. In the summer before college, I made up my mind to become a minister. I truly believed that to serve God was the highest calling. Of course, when I review that decision with a better understanding of psychological motivations, I recognize that there were probably other factors as well. Although my parents put no pressure on me, I knew this decision would please them. I also admired some preachers; their speaking ability and personality were impressive. One of my older cousins, Charles "Abe" Lincoln, talked to me at this time and encouraged me to be a minister. Abe was a star football player and had decided to become a minister. Naturally, a young man of this stature could make a strong impression on me. So I was happy with my decision and headed off to ACC to complete my education as a ministerial student.

At that time, I had rarely questioned the fundamental tenets of my culture and the belief system in which I was raised. Why would I? It was the only thing I knew, and it had served me well. It was only later that I began to realize that my contentment was based partly on the fact that I was a White male born into a relatively affluent, well-educated family. For many in the citizenry of Sweetwater, this wasn't the case. It was only after I left that town that I began to realize some of the serious flaws of the culture I grew up in.

Sweetwater, like all places in Texas, was segregated. African Americans—"colored people," as they were called at the time—could not attend our schools. They could not eat in "White restaurants"; they would have been refused if they'd tried. Blacks lived in the poorer section of town, since they could only get menial jobs. Since African Americans were a small proportion of our town, I don't recall any racial strife or any Whites organizing a chapter of the Ku Klux Klan. The discrimination was more covert but clearly understood. It took me some time to realize how shamefully the African Americans were treated. I have often thought how different my life would have been if I had been born Black instead of White. I would have been denied good schooling, been refused entrance to stores, and probably never gone to college.

Although less harsh, another form of discrimination practiced in Sweetwater was gender based. Patriarchy was the rule, and men were considered the head of the household. Women were largely dependent on marriage for economic security. If women worked, they were generally restricted to occupations such as nurses, teachers, or retail clerks. There were no female lawyers or doctors. All the civic clubs, such as the Lions Club, were strictly male. It was an unwritten rule in our high school that boys were the class presidents. Girls were normally the class secretaries. All this was just accepted; I don't recall conversations about gender discrimination. It would take time, life experience, and serious thought for me to radically change my views on these significant cultural issues.

CHAPTER 3

A Time to Enjoy, A Time to Love

(1950–1957)

Figure 3.1. Jack as a college senior, 1954

Figure 3.2. Jack and Lacreta's wedding, September 2, 1954

Abilene lies in the flat land of West Texas. It is often called Big Country, since the blue sky seems to reach up to heaven. The town originated in the 1880s as a cattle stop on the Texas and Pacific Railroad, and it grew steadily in the decades that followed. When the army base Camp Barkeley was built there during World War II, the population later doubled as many soldiers returned to the area after the war. By the time I started college in Abilene in 1950, the population was forty-five thousand and would double again within the decade. For a boy from Sweetwater, Abilene was the big city.

Abilene Christian College (ACC) was a Christian liberal arts college of 1,500 students when I began there. I was familiar with the campus, since my father had taken me there many times to attend athletic events and other activities. I was very excited on the day my parents drove me to ACC to enroll. My parents drove me up to Barracks 9, where I would be living, and we unpacked my belongings. At this time, male students were housed in remodeled barracks that ACC had purchased from the US Army after World War II. In my freshman year, I roomed with Don Faver, an older cousin of mine, who was a senior at the college. Our room had a bunk bed, a closet, a table, and two chairs. Across the hall from us were a communal restroom and showers.

Despite these sparse accommodations, I was happy and began to form friendships with many of the boys in the barracks. I recall having long conversations (called bull sessions) in the evening and playing dominoes and board games after class. We college boys also enjoyed playing pranks on one another. I must admit to enjoying this activity. However, on one occasion, playing a prank almost got me in trouble. I had filled a balloon with water, sneaked into a friend's room, and placed the balloon over his door. I then placed a pin on the door so that when my friend opened it, the pin would pierce the balloon and drench him with water. I was awaiting my friend's return when suddenly, the dorm supervisor appeared to do a room inspection. At the sight of him, I hastily departed to the library for a few hours. Upon my return, I learned that the supervisor had been thoroughly drenched when he opened my friend's door, but fortunately, he did not learn the identity of the prankster.

I primarily enrolled in required general education courses in science, math, English, and history my freshman year. I also began my studies in the Bible Department that year. I was one of several hundred young men who were ministerial students at the college, and a Bible major was recommended. In addition to my studies, there were ample opportunities for enjoyment on campus, such as intramural sports, musical and drama events, and a recreation center. I often visited the recreation center, where I talked with friends, watched television, and played many games of Ping-Pong. I also was on an intramural touch football team during my four years in college. Dancing or drinking alcoholic beverages, however, was not permitted on campus. Since I had not engaged in these activities in high school, I felt no great sense of deprivation.

One highlight of the year was the huge bonfire built before the annual homecoming football game. I am not exaggerating in using the term *huge*. Imagine four telephone poles encased in wire with an area at the bottom of 25 × 25 feet. We college boys would work on and off for a week to fill this space to the very top with old tires, discarded furniture, and all kinds of rubbish. The girls in the dormitories would bring us doughnuts and coffee for an hour in the evening while we worked. Then the night before the big game, we would gather around to watch the bonfire burn. Some years later, the college wisely abandoned this practice because of its danger and possible fire hazard. At the time, though, I found the bonfire very exciting.

One extracurricular activity that was very important to me was debate. I had participated in debate in my high school years, and I continued to enjoy it in college. Our debate team traveled to several college tournaments, and my partner and I generally did well in this competition. This experience sharpened my speaking skills as well as my ability to think quickly on my feet. Both of these skills would prove invaluable in my later career.

During that year, a conversation with Paul Earnhart, a fellow debater and a sophomore at ACC, proved very significant in my life. Since our debates involved national issues, it was natural that these issues would also come up in private conversation. When the subject of race arose, Paul strongly expressed his view that segregation was an evil practice. At first, I questioned Paul's view. I had grown up in a segregated town and had little contact with African Americans. Though my parents had not expressed any hatred of Blacks, they had accepted the status quo of Texas culture, and so had I. But after my conversation with Paul, I began to realize I was wrong. I reflected on Jesus's simple statement "And as you wish that men would do to you, do so to them" (Luke 6:31). In my heart, I knew that I would not want to be treated as African Americans were treated. So I did a 180-degree turn. I realized that my own college was absolutely wrong in denying admission to African Americans. I began to freely express my belief in racial equality, which resulted in many long discussions with family members and friends.

Words do matter; that thoughtful conversation made a real difference. The seed that initial conversation had planted would grow in me. Racial equality became a very important issue in my life. This was a significant turning point for me because it was the first time I seriously questioned my culture. It opened the possibility that my previously held views could be wrong. Since my church practiced segregation, could some of their other religious views also be open to question? This was only a small crack in changing my worldview, but it began a pattern in my life. I became open to changing my views if truth led me there, for truth was very important to me. As Jesus once declared, "You will know the truth, and the truth will make you free" (John 8:32).

A rather strange incident also happened in my freshman year. Like many ACC students, I generally attended our football games. One night, I was at a game with my younger cousin, Altus Scott. I was proudly wearing a shirt, formerly owned by my brother, that had the ACC wildcat mascot emblazoned on it. We had just defeated our crosstown rival, McMurry College. Altus and I were leaving the game to get into his parents' car when we were suddenly confronted by three young men who were clearly not happy with the outcome of the game. I tried to calm the leader's taunts, but without success. He suddenly struck me in the face with his fist. I quickly responded by grabbing him around the waist, throwing him to the ground, and landing astride him. Just then, a police officer ran up and broke up the fight. I quickly stood up and told the officer that my opponent had initiated the fight. My uncle Crutcher, Altus's father, backed me up. The officer allowed us to leave. As we left, I saw the police officer sternly lecturing the young man who had hit me. I realized I was lucky; if the officer had not arrived, the two other young men might have jumped in to aid their defeated companion. It could have ended very badly. Fortunately, this encounter was the last physical conflict I ever had. My future conflicts would be restricted only to those of a verbal nature.

I returned to my parents' home in Sweetwater in the summer of 1951, after my freshman year. I was fortunate to land a job on the Texas and Pacific Railroad that summer and for two summers thereafter. My work involved unloading boxcars filled with merchandise that was destined for the stores in Sweetwater. An experienced man and I unloaded this merchandise with hand trucks beginning at four in the morning. These goods needed to be on the dock and properly sorted by the time the truck drivers arrived at seven o'clock. I would then have a lighter load for the rest of the morning and finish my eight-hour shift by noon. I was paid the lordly sum of one dollar per hour, which was not bad for that time. It was also an opportunity for me to work with laborers, to interact with them and learn more about their work and home life. I respected their manual labor and realized they did not have the privileges that I had. I might add that their language was far saltier than what I heard at home or at my college.

That summer also gave me the opportunity to gain practical experience in being a minister. I began my work as what was called a "preacher boy." There was a practice at ACC that some of the ministerial students would drive out on Sundays and preach at small rural churches. These churches could not support a full-time minister but could give a stipend to a student. Of course, this was an excellent opportunity for young men to develop their preaching skills. In retrospect, I have often wondered how patient some of those people must have been to listen to eighteen- to twenty-one-year-old men make religious pronouncements Sunday after Sunday.

There was a Church of Christ in Noodle, a community only about thirty miles west of Abilene. A professor at ACC was their regular preacher, but he was to be away that summer. I was able to be his replacement for the months he was gone. This experience opened the door for me to be a regular preacher for the rest of my college career. In my sophomore year, I was the preacher at Herndon Chapel, twenty-five miles north of Abilene. Then in my junior year, I returned to Noodle and preached for that church until I graduated from college.

There was a regular rhythm in my work with these churches. I would preach on both Sunday mornings and Sunday evenings. On Sunday afternoons, I would eat lunch in one of the members' homes. The women of the church would make a list of who would host the preacher each Sunday. These lunches were more like dinners, and as a hungry college boy, I delighted in these meals. They were often the culinary highlight of my week. However, one Sunday after enjoying a delicious lunch with a church family in Noodle, a funny mishap occurred. I always enjoyed playing with children, and that Sunday, I was roughhousing with boys from the family and church, three or four of them, aged about eight to twelve. I was only about nineteen myself. I was wearing my lightweight, blue-striped, white seersucker suit, traditionally worn in the South in summer. In the course of our rough-and-tumble play, the crotch seam of my suit pants split open, leaving me with a very embarrassing rip. The concerned wife of the family quickly ushered me to a bedroom, where I removed my pants and handed them through the door to her. I sat there in my underwear for about thirty minutes while she sewed my pants back up. I was relieved when I heard the knock on the door that announced my pants were once again presentable. I wore those pants when I preached again that evening, just happy that the congregation wouldn't be getting to know me a little too well!

Since these churches were close to Abilene, I would also return on Wednesday evenings to teach a Bible class. I remember receiving thirty dollars weekly, which in the early 1950s was a decided help on college expenses. All this traveling meant that I needed a car. Since my preaching contributed to my college expenses, my father surprised me by buying me a new car to replace my used car in my junior year. An added benefit was that the new car improved my dating chances.

In my junior year, several important events occurred that had decided effects on my future. The first was the presidential election of 1952, pitting Adlai Stevenson against Dwight Eisenhower. The college decided to have a parallel campus debate on this election. A psychology professor, a student, and I represented Stevenson, whereas an education professor and two other students represented Eisenhower. The debate was widely advertised and well attended. As in most debates, the attendees probably decided that the victors were the persons supporting the candidate whom they had already determined to vote for in the coming election.

This debate raised an important question for me: Why was I a Democrat? My choice was significant, since it would have a tremendous impact on my future. Admittedly, the first reason that I was a Democrat was that my father was a Democrat. He was a New Deal Democrat who had served two terms in the Texas House of Representatives. He was a vocal supporter of Franklin Roosevelt, believing that President Roosevelt had stood up for the common people. He would cite measures such as Social Security and rural electrification as evidence for his political convictions. His arguments made sense to me, and I would later see issues such as civil rights, Medicare, and health care as continuing this Democratic tradition of seeking the common good. That does not mean that I believe that any political party, nation, or individual is always right. But through the years, I have not found reason to change my political leanings.

In the spring of 1953, I decided to seek the office of student body president for the following school year. Quite a number of students encouraged me to do this. I had been elected to the house of representatives in my sophomore year. My speaking skills, sharpened by debate and preaching, aided me in this pursuit. Once I decided to run, I threw all my energy into winning the election. I asked key students to solicit votes for me. Each directed their efforts at certain segments of the student body: men's and women's dormitories, athletic teams, social clubs, agricultural students, and so on. One custom at the college was for candidates to have displays outside the daily morning chapel. Frequently, these displays had a humorous twist. One day, I had two guys asleep in a bunk bed with a large sign declaring, "We are sleeping for Jack Scott while he works day and night for good student government." The next day, I had a country music band composed of students playing on a flatbed truck while a friend, Andy Nelson, imitated a former Texas governor, W. Lee O'Daniel. He loudly extolled my virtues. Corny? Probably. However, I beat my opponent, Gary Freeman, by a margin of 2–1 with about one thousand votes cast.

Serving as student body president in my senior year was a great learning experience. I met weekly with a cabinet of student leaders that included the vice president and secretary of the student body, plus the presidents of the freshman, sophomore, junior, and senior classes. On occasion, I would preside over a meeting of the entire student body. I learned how to work with a group of people to get things done. For instance, in the fall, I had the idea to charter a train to Wichita Falls for a football game between ACC and Midwestern University. So I contacted the Santa Fe Railroad officials about this possibility. After determining the cost, I then sold the idea to administration officials at the college. We next had to price the tickets and make sure that enough students bought the tickets to ensure a profit for the railroad. Fortunately, the plan worked. The students had a ball taking a round trip on the train, and we even topped it off by ACC winning the football game. I enjoyed being a leader, and my success was a boost to my self-confidence.

Important as all of this was, the most life-changing event of the spring semester occurred on April 9, 1953. That was my first date with Lacreta Isbell, who eventually became my wife. I had noticed her when she arrived as a freshman in the fall of 1952. I recall seeing her in an orange knit suit, standing at the front of the auditorium after chapel. She filled out the orange suit perfectly. Lacreta was strikingly beautiful. Her shiny brown hair curled softly above her shoulders, and her eyes were teal blue with just a hint of green. When Lacreta smiled, her face was radiant, and people smiled with her.

Of course, her date calendar filled quickly, and soon Lacreta was going steady with a student named Kenneth Helterbrand. After a few months, they broke up, and I began thinking about calling her for a date. I waited a while to make sure that this breakup was permanent. Finally, the time was right. I was invited to the band banquet, since I had served as their master of ceremonies on their recent tour. So I got up my nerve and called Lacreta to go as my date. To my happiness and relief, she agreed.

After a few dates, I was smitten. I discovered that Lacreta was not only beautiful but also very intelligent. She had been the valedictorian of her graduating class in Elk City, Oklahoma. We had great conversations as we got to know each other. We shared religious views; she was supportive of my desire to be a minister. After all, her father was a Church of Christ minister, so she knew the joys and sacrifices of this calling. Furthermore, my parents were impressed when I introduced Lacreta to them. She was definitely a "keeper."

It was not long after I started dating Lacreta that I began to realize she was the woman whom I wanted to marry. And if there is one trait I have, it is that when I establish an important goal, I pursue it relentlessly. So I made courting and eventually marrying Lacreta my number one priority. In the summer of 1953, she stayed in Abilene between school years to work full-time in a department store. I would often work on my railroad job, which finished at noon; drive the forty-mile trip to Abilene in the late afternoon to pick her up when she got off work; and spend the evening with her. I would return to Sweetwater after midnight, sleep a

Figure 3.3. Jack Scott, Outstanding Male Graduate at Abilene Christian College, 1954

few hours, and go to work at four o'clock. I was young and in love, and I considered sleeping overrated when I could be with Lacreta. I still cherish a memorable image from that summer of Lacreta, in a flower-sprigged dress, glowing with happiness as she rushed into my arms to greet me.

I wasn't the only one in the family falling in love. In the summer of 1953, my sister, Patsy, married Foy Vinson in the Sweetwater Church of Christ. They had begun dating in Patsy's freshman year. They fell in love and were married after Foy's graduation. Foy was a minister; Patsy a devoted homemaker and life partner.

When the 1953–54 school year began, Lacreta and I were constantly together. We sat together in daily chapel. I would take her to work in the department store on weekday afternoons and pick her up after work. We were passionately in love. For some time, I wanted to ask Lacreta to marry me, but first, I wanted to be sure of her feelings. When I felt the time was right, I scraped together $300 in cash and purchased an engagement ring. Nine months after we started dating, on January 4, 1954, I proposed to Lacreta. We had dinner at the café across the street from the campus that evening. Afterward, I drove to a secluded spot near the college library. I parked the car, turned to her, and told her how much I loved her. I told her that I wanted to marry her and showed her the ring. She responded just as I had hoped. She was thrilled with the ring and quickly said yes.

Now she and I wanted everyone to know that we were engaged. The next day, we proudly announced our engagement to the world. I doubt that anyone was surprised, but they certainly were happy for us.

In May of 1954, I graduated from ACC with a bachelor's degree and was honored as the Outstanding Male Graduate. I have happy memories of my years at the college. I made many friends, some of whom became lifetime friends. Among them were Gary Freeman, Jon Jones, Dwain Evans, Houston Goodspeed, and Jim Wilburn. And my educational horizons were broadened. I particularly recall the influence of one professor, Dr. Frank Pack. Dr. Pack was a gifted, knowledgeable professor with a depth and polish that caused him to stand out. He was the first person to say to me, "Jack, you ought to go to graduate school." My original plan was to get my bachelor's degree and then begin my ministerial career. But by the end of college, I began to think about being a religion professor myself.

Of course, of all my college memories, the happiest is finding Lacreta. We decided to get married at the end of the summer. Her parents agreed to this, although I am sure they had reservations about Lacreta marrying before finishing college. Her parents were moving to Midland, Texas, where her father was to be the minister of the Church of Christ there. So we determined that the wedding would occur there on September 2.

I had landed a job with ACC to travel throughout Texas and recruit students that summer. Of course, I would also need a job after Lacreta and I were married. After scouting out several possibilities, I accepted the offer to be the minister of the Church of Christ in Graford, Texas, beginning after our marriage. Graford was a small town located about one hundred miles east of Abilene. If, by this time, you have surmised that I am an inveterate planner for the future, I plead guilty.

I completed my job with ACC that summer and stopped by my home in Sweetwater before leaving for Midland for my wedding. As I lay in bed on that final night at home, I was deeply touched by an action of my father. He came into the room and embraced me, with tears streaming down his face. He knew that I was leaving home for good to start my own family. The last chapter of childhood was over. And for a man who seldom cried, his expression of such love for me was very moving. My father will always be one of my heroes. I could not have asked for a better father and role model.

The next day, I traveled to Midland for the big event. We had asked Don Morris, the president of ACC, to officiate at the wedding. My brother, Morris, was the best man, and Fran Boren, Lacreta's roommate in college, was the maid of honor. Lacreta looked beautiful in a creamy white wedding dress with long lace sleeves, her hair crowned by a headpiece and simple veil. As she walked down the aisle, I thought about how blessed I was. In photos of that day, it is obvious how joyful we were. In our sixty-six years of marriage, that feeling never really went away. Lacreta was as beautiful to me in her last days on earth as she was on our wedding day.

We left after the wedding for our honeymoon. We had rented a cabin near Glenwood Springs, Colorado, for several days. We were ecstatic to be married and enjoyed a variety of experiences: horseback riding, movies, eating at unusual restaurants, and visiting sites in Colorado. But the biggest joy was being together and realizing we had made a lifetime commitment.

We moved to Graford in mid-September, and I took up the role of minister of the church. The first week was marked by the church giving us newlyweds a shower, which included such things as groceries, kitchen utensils, and household goods. Other than preaching and teaching, I spent time getting acquainted with church members, visiting the sick, meeting people in this small town, and dealing in general with church business.

One of the benefits of the ministerial life was the lessons I learned in close interactions with people. People would share their problems with me, even though my youth did not suggest that I had a depth of wisdom. I recall visiting with a woman suffering from terminal cancer. On one occasion, she shared the fact that her family had placed her medicine away from her bed, lest in extreme pain she would take an overdose in order to die. Perhaps my prayers and sympathy were of some help.

Another lesson I learned was that disaster does not necessarily bring one to repentance. One of the women of the church had a son who drank heavily and was living a dissolute life. Then he was in a serious car accident that almost killed him and resulted in a long hospital stay, leaving him on crutches for some time afterward. I naively pictured the man following the biblical example of the prodigal son, who came to his senses and repented. Not so with this young man. As soon as he recovered, he returned to his former lifestyle. Experiences like these were learning moments for me.

A few months after we arrived in Graford, we discovered that Lacreta was pregnant. We were excited and proudly announced her pregnancy when we visited both parents' homes at Christmastime. However, soon after Christmas, Lacreta began to experience extreme nausea. Her inability to hold down food led to her losing twenty pounds. Finally, she was admitted to the nearest hospital, in Mineral Wells, for intravenous feeding. The attending doctor even mentioned the possibility of a therapeutic abortion if they could not stop the nausea. Naturally, I would have permitted this surgery in order to save Lacreta's life. Fortunately, she recovered. After her release from the hospital, I took Lacreta to her grandparents' home in Fort Worth for a few weeks of rest and full recovery.

Our stay in Graford was not long. Don Morris called in the summer of 1955 and offered me a position as assistant to the president at ACC. Naturally, I was flattered, since I had desired to return to my alma mater one day. This position involved general public relations, fundraising, contacts with alumni, and other miscellaneous duties. I worked in the Development Office with Bill Teague (a later president of the college), Jon Jones (a good friend), and Joyce Whitefield. Joyce was a funny, extremely capable woman who would have advanced even further if the "glass ceiling" hindering female advancement had not been in place.

On August 12, 1955, shortly after moving to Abilene, we were blessed with a beautiful, healthy baby girl. We named her Sharon Lacreta. We delighted in Sharon; we naturally thought she was the most beautiful of all babies. Then on November 17, 1956, Sheila was born. She, too, was a delight. Lacreta was an excellent mother. She'd had the experience in high school of helping her mother care for two much younger siblings (Mary Sue, fourteen years younger, and John Paul, seventeen years younger). I had always enjoyed playing with small children, so I happily embraced fatherhood. However, I freely admit that the parenting responsibility largely fell on Lacreta's shoulders.

I was rather successful in fundraising, and in my second year in the Development Office at ACC, I was given the added responsibility of alumni secretary. This involved considerable traveling. I enjoyed the travel, although I missed the family. Sometimes I would drop in on fellow classmates. I also enjoyed fitting in track meets on my travels. This was the era when ACC had a great track team, headed by the world-famous sprinter Bobby Morrow. Morrow won the one-hundred- and two-hundred-meter races in the 1956 Olympics in Melbourne, Australia. Lacreta and I had traveled with my brother, Morris, and his wife, Estelle, and another couple to attend the Olympic trials in Los Angeles. We cheered Morrow on as he won both the one-hundred- and two-hundred-meter races to qualify for the Olympics.

In addition to my job at ACC, I often preached on Sundays to fill in for ministers who were away or, in some instances, at churches where there were several-month gaps between the departure of one minister and the arrival of another. One such congregation was the Birdville Church of Christ in Fort Worth. In the months that I was there, I must have made a good impression. One of the elders, Monroe Brown, commented that if I ever chose to do mission work, that church might be willing to sponsor me. I thanked him and simply said that I might consider it.

However, at this time, I had a less positive experience in my preaching. I had been invited to preach at the Sunday service of my home congregation in Sweetwater. During the week before I was scheduled to preach, I had been sick with what I thought was the flu. I began to recover and believed I could still preach on that Sunday. Lacreta advised me to postpone the engagement, but a young man in his twenties is not easily deterred.

So we drove from Abilene to Sweetwater, and at the appointed time, I stepped forward to the pulpit and began my sermon. But about ten minutes into my sermon, I began to feel dizzy. The next thing I knew, I fainted and fell over backward, flat on my back. When I woke up, I was surrounded by the faces of several men, looking down at me with concern. I feebly suggested I could continue with my sermon, but the men wisely disagreed, helping me to my feet and guiding me to my seat. The audience, containing some of my family and friends, was naturally frightened and concerned, particularly Lacreta. Within a short time, fortunately, I felt much better. However, when I saw a doctor upon returning to Abilene, I discovered I had pneumonia. I was given medication and confined to bed until I recovered. Happily, I never repeated that rather dramatic performance in the many sermons I preached afterward. Zane Reeves, who became a good friend of mine years later at Pepperdine, was a young boy in the Sweetwater church on the day I keeled over. He would often teasingly remind me of that memorable occasion.

I enjoyed my work at ACC, and I believe that I could have made a career as an administrator at the college. But after my college graduation, I had earned eighteen hours of graduate credits at the college toward a master's degree in Bible. I still harbored the desire to be a professor of religion, and I knew that eventually, I would want a PhD degree to fulfill this ambition. Things would shortly happen that would move me in that direction.

Early in 1957, I heard of a small church in New Haven, Connecticut, that was looking for a preacher. Since Churches of Christ had few congregations in New England, New Haven was considered a mission field. Furthermore, New Haven was the home of Yale University, and Yale had a highly respected Divinity School. I began to think seriously about relocating there. First, the idea of doing mission work appealed to me. To take a small church, add members through teaching the Bible, and live in another section of the country were all exciting to me. And the possibility of pursuing a graduate degree at Yale Divinity School (YDS) interested me greatly. I felt strongly that this opportunity was

God's calling. Lacreta and I had extensive conversations about this matter. It was no small consideration for her to leave family and friends and move across the country with two children. Lacreta, however, was up for the adventure and supported me in whatever way she could. So I contacted the Birdville Church of Christ to ask if they were still interested in supporting me in mission work. Fortunately, they were. Not everyone was enthusiastic about my plans. Some at ACC warned me that YDS was liberal and that studying in a university like that would be harmful to my faith. At that time, ACC had a course entitled "The Bible vs. Modernism" that warned of the dangers of liberalism. I, too, shared those conservative views. Yet I was confident that I could maintain my faith and still profit from additional education. After all, there were Bible teachers at ACC who had doctoral degrees in religion from liberal universities. LeMoine Lewis, from Harvard, and J. D. Thomas, from the University of Chicago, were two such examples.

There was one other piece added to the possibilities in New Haven. I learned that there was also a small church in Groton, Connecticut, that was looking for a preacher. A large church in Madison, Tennessee, had promised to support this church. Groton was only fifty miles east of New Haven. I contacted my close friend, Gary Freeman, who was the minister of the Church of Christ in Clarksville, Texas, to encourage him and his wife, Betty, to consider the opportunity in Groton. Gary and I had formed a close friendship in our senior year in college. We discovered a commonality in long conversations about life in general and religion in particular. We also shared many moments of humor; Gary was one of the funniest persons I had ever known. Our friendship was also strengthened by the fact that our wives, Lacreta and Betty, had been close friends for their two years in college. And after our respective marriages, we had maintained that close relationship as couples. So the Freemans were very interested in the Groton opportunity.

The result was that in the summer of 1957, the Scotts and Freemans took an exploratory trip to Connecticut. We were both excited, and the trip itself was most enjoyable. For instance, we traveled through the

Great Smoky Mountains and attended our first major league baseball game at Yankee Stadium in New York City. None of us had been to the Northeast; visiting a vibrant city like New York was a grand adventure. Then Gary and I preached at the respective churches in New Haven and Groton. Both churches were enthusiastic about our moving there and becoming their ministers. Importantly, we had already secured support for our salaries, which was essential to these small churches.

Naturally, neither my nor Lacreta's parents were overly enthusiastic about this move, since they would miss us and the children. ACC also tried to dissuade me from leaving. But Lacreta and I had given much thought and prayer to the decision. So in October of 1957, we packed up our belongings, along with our two small daughters, and headed for New Haven. Thus began a new chapter for us, the beginning of a journey that would change our lives in ways we never imagined.

CHAPTER 4

A Time to Plant, A Time to Learn

(1957–1962)

Figure 4.1. Jack and Lacreta with family, 1960

Figure 4.2. Sharon's first day of school, standing on the porch of the Church of Christ, New Haven, 1961

Unlike my ancestors, my pioneering journey was heading east rather than west. After leaving Abilene, we were able to see many more trees and mountains than on the flat plains of West Texas. It was a long journey from Texas to Connecticut, through cities and countryside. The final leg of our journey was from New York City to New Haven. As we traveled the Merritt Parkway in Connecticut on our way to New Haven, we were struck with the sheer beauty of the fall leaves along the way. This was a nice introduction to our new home.

We settled into a motel, staying there until we could locate a house to rent. Soon we found a nice Cape Cod three-bedroom house in North Haven.

The church regularly met on Sunday mornings in a rented space at the West Haven Community House. I preached my first sermon there on October 6, 1957. At that time, the church numbered about twenty-five members.

As I began this ministry, I considered what steps I should take to assist this small church. As always, I discussed these plans with Lacreta; we truly viewed this as a joint venture. We also prayed that God would continue to give us guidance in this challenging undertaking.

First, I knew I needed to get to know the church members and assess their strengths and abilities as we worked together. They were a diverse group. About one-third of the congregation was African American. This pleased me, since the lack of integrated churches in Texas had distressed me. Also, these members could open the door to working in the African American community. Others in the church were native southerners. They had already been members of Churches of Christ when they moved to the New Haven area as a result of marriage or job location. I recall two young women, Peggy Shia and Betty Brown, who were very dedicated members. They had met their husbands during World War II. After marriage, they had moved to the area, since their husbands were natives of the region. These two women attended and served the church faithfully. Other members were students at Yale. For example, Herbert Goertz was a native German who was in the PhD program in economics at Yale. He was the church treasurer and would become a close friend. Our many conversations together broadened my knowledge; I learned from his advanced education and international experience. And some members of the congregation were natives of the area who had been baptized and become members of the church. Lacreta and I would often visit in the homes of all the members and also invite them to our home. Lacreta was very hospitable and an excellent cook, so this became a way to form friendships. It also laid the groundwork to discuss ideas to help the church grow.

A second step was to reach out and bring in new members to the church. I believed that our message of restoring New Testament Christianity was appealing. And as early Christians had practiced, I believed in teaching the good news so that persons could receive forgiveness of sins and live the Christian life. I believed that an effective method to bring in new members would be for our present members to invite their friends to church. Another approach would be for members to invite persons to their homes for a Bible study. I would conduct the study, which could lead people to be baptized and become members of the church. Although anyone was welcome to attend the church, only those who stated their faith in Jesus Christ and were baptized could be members.

At this time, Churches of Christ had a national television program called the *Herald of Truth*. The main feature of this program was a sermon presented by an effective minister. At the end of the program, listeners were encouraged to send in requests for more information. The *Herald of Truth* would then send them information about the Church of Christ and answer their questions. This program would also send the name and address of those requesting this information to the nearest congregation.

When I received these names, I would follow up and call on the individual requesting information. Some of these calls were fruitful. For instance, Ruth Oemcke saw the *Herald of Truth* and requested more information about the Church of Christ. I went to her home in nearby Beacon Falls and met with her and her husband, Ludwig. After a period of Bible study, they both were baptized and became faithful members of our church. On another occasion, I met and taught three adults who had a background with Jehovah's Witnesses. They had become disenchanted with that organization. After several visits, they were converted and became members of our church.

Occasionally, visits resulting from the responses to the *Herald of Truth* were rather strange encounters. On one visit, I was accompanied by Dale Combs, a church member. We went to the house of a man who talked to us on his front porch. Soon we were joined by his friend, an African American woman who was a Pentecostal preacher. She began to preach to us in a loud voice, proclaiming her ability to perform miracles as the apostles did. Thinking to challenge her, I asked if she could raise the dead as Jesus and the apostles had. Undaunted, she claimed she could. As she continued her rant, Dale worked hard to stifle his laughter. Misinterpreting his smiling face as an openness to receive the Holy Spirit, she stated he was about "to get the Spirit." But turning toward my stern face, she proclaimed that I was not.

I visited in the homes of people from all walks of life. Sometimes I would call on those who lived in the tenement areas. I recall meeting with Alberta Smith. She and her family had moved to New Haven from Maine in order to find work. She was a member of the Church of Christ and began attending our church. Eventually, her two sisters, Phyliss and Rachel, were baptized. In this work, I learned a great deal about people in general and about their religious thinking in particular. I discussed the Bible with Mormons, Jehovah's Witnesses, Catholics, and others. It was quite a learning experience.

I also worked in the African American community. One African American church member was Essie Felder. We were able to baptize her sister-in-law, Isabel Hilton, and later we baptized two daughters of these women, who then became members of the church. When we began conducting Vacation Bible Schools in the summers, it brought in many children from the African American community. Later one of my professors at the Divinity School, Harry Baker Adams, visited our church. He was very impressed with the successful integration of our church, since most of the White churches in the New Haven area had not been successful in their efforts to attract African Americans to their churches.

Another way we gained members was that I encouraged young, zealous members of Churches of Christ in Texas and neighboring states to move to New Haven to help this small, struggling church. This had led to the migration of Dale Combs and Nellis Williams, recent graduates of Harding College. Both of these young men were most helpful. Dale spent most of the rest of his life in the New Haven area as a high school biology teacher. Later he was instrumental in planting another church in neighboring Wallingford. Another helpful addition was Seymour and Kay Evans from the Broadway Church of Christ in Lubbock, Texas. They stayed in our home until they located an apartment. They attended our church faithfully and were encouraging to other members.

Then on one of my trips to Texas, I dropped by Abilene Christian College (ACC). I talked with Paul Watson, a Bible major who graduated as valedictorian of his 1961 class. He was planning to get his PhD from Harvard, but I talked to him about coming to Yale. I pointed out there were already several Church of Christ graduate religion students at Harvard, but none other than myself at Yale. So Paul and Ann Watson moved to New Haven and immediately became central at our church. In time, he followed me as minister of the church when I left in 1962. Paul proved to be a very effective minister. He eventually got a doctorate in religion from Yale University. He taught in several colleges but eventually had a long and fruitful ministry in the Church of Christ in Durham, North Carolina.

All these dedicated and talented people were a real boost to this church. They invited people to church, and the men led worship in song and prayer, even preaching in my absence. Lacreta and I helped them by bringing them into our home when they arrived and sharing our knowledge of the area as they got settled. They also became close friends.

Obviously, there is a strong bond formed as people share a common goal together.

From the beginning of this ministry, I realized we could not meet in a community center forever. I knew that to aid growth and establish permanence for this church, it would be necessary to construct a church building. This would be no small undertaking, since the church owned no land, nor did it possess any funds to construct a building.

Once again, Lacreta and I developed a strategy. The first step that we took was to create a monthly newsletter describing the progress of the church. This was sent not only to churches already supporting the work but also to churches and individuals who might later donate to the construction of a building.

After being in New Haven for a year and experiencing a steady growth in membership, I believed that I could visit interested churches in Texas and neighboring states to raise money for a building fund. We prepared an attractive brochure that detailed the history of this church, the prospects for growth in the future, the need for a church building, and the estimated costs of a building. In the fall of 1958, I spent two months traveling to churches and key individuals to sell this project. I was successful in raising sufficient money to purchase a site for a church building. This was my first experience in raising funds for a building project, something that would prove useful later in my career.

After looking at several sites, we found an ideal location in Hamden, a suburb north of New Haven. It was located on Whitney Avenue, a main thoroughfare, and there was sufficient space for both the building and parking. Furthermore, there was an older home on the property that, after slight remodeling, could serve as a parsonage. Our family spent our last two years there, thus saving the church the cost of renting a home for us.

In early 1960, we signed a contract with Paden Construction Company, which had constructed many buildings for Churches of Christ throughout the nation. We were blessed in financing this building. Thomas and Lynette Brown loaned us $50,000 at a reasonable rate for a twenty-year mortgage. Lynette was a member of the church, and Tom was the first person to be baptized after the new building opened. The building was formally dedicated on September 11, 1960. It was an attractive red brick building with an auditorium seating about 150 people. It had a full basement, with Sunday school rooms, a kitchen with space for a gathering, and an office. The mortgage was paid off on schedule, and this building has continued to serve this church for over sixty years.

In this new building, the church continued to grow to about eighty to eighty-five members, and on some occasions, our Sunday morning attendance grew to over one hundred. I continued in my ministerial role (preaching, counseling, and overseeing the general operation of the church) until our departure in 1962.

Though I was dedicated to the growth and nurturing of the church, it was not the only reason Lacreta and I had moved to New Haven. I also wanted the opportunity to receive an advanced degree in religion from Yale Divinity School (YDS). I had not chosen to enroll in the first two years we lived in New Haven, choosing rather to concentrate on my work with the church. But in the spring of 1959, I applied for admission to YDS. I took the Graduate Record Exam (GRE) and, fortunately, scored well on this exam. In my application, I included my score on the GRE and my transcript from ACC. I was accepted, and I began my study for the three-year master of divinity degree in the fall.

As is natural in any new undertaking, I had some anxieties. Many of the entering students had bachelor's degrees from much more prestigious colleges than ACC. Would I not be as well prepared as other students? How well would I adapt, since I was the only student from the Church of Christ? Yet I was also excited about this new adventure. After a few months, I was convinced that I could meet the academic standards. And I truly found both the professors and the course of study very interesting and challenging.

Some learning experiences result in your questions being answered; others result in your answers being questioned. It was the latter that occurred for me at YDS. Slowly over this three-year period, I began to rethink some of my previous religious positions. For instance, in my first year at YDS, I thoroughly enjoyed the church history class taught by the renowned scholar Roland Bainton. He was known for his seminal biography of Martin Luther, *Here I Stand.* As I studied the life of Francis of Assisi in Professor Bainton's class, I was deeply impressed by his sacrificial love for the poor, such as care for the lepers. Had not Jesus in Matthew 25 pictured the final judgment scene as being determined by whether one fed the hungry, visited the sick, clothed the naked, and so on? Yes, Francis was a Catholic monk, but was he denied heaven because some of his doctrines were incorrect? He seemed to be following the teachings of Jesus more closely than many of my fellow Christians in the Church of Christ.

In Churches of Christ at this time, the Catholic Church was roundly denounced; the entire medieval period was considered to be one giant apostasy. Yet I was enriched by reading from Catholic authors such as Augustine and Thomas Aquinas from the medieval period. Even today, I enjoy reading from contemporary Catholic authors, such as Richard Rohr, Thomas Merton, and Sister Helen Prejean. I still did not believe in Catholic doctrines such as the infallibility of the papacy, the enforced celibacy of the priesthood, or praying to the saints. But I realized I had previously lived in a religious cocoon that had led me to resist many insights to be gained from the teachings and practices of other religious bodies. After all, I reasoned, we in Churches of Christ had been enriched by singing hymns written by members of other churches. Couldn't we also profit from reading books written by authors from other churches or perhaps even listening to their sermons?

I also began to realize that in my past defense of the Bible, I had felt compelled to defend its scientific accuracy. In my childhood, I had even wondered if I could believe in dinosaurs, since the Bible never mentioned them. I gradually began to realize that the Bible is not a scientific textbook; it is a spiritual guide written in the context of that time. For instance, did the sun stand still, as described in Joshua 10:13, or is this the Israelites' understanding of what God miraculously did in aiding them to win that battle? Also, why get into an argument over the geological age of the earth? Why not affirm instead that God created the heavens and the earth? And if that process took billions of years, why try to force the "days" of Genesis to be twenty-four-hour periods?

This did not mean I automatically accepted every claim by a scientist. For instance, I still believe that the scientist who claims there is no God has gone beyond the scope of science. It takes a great leap of faith to believe that matter is eternal and that the universe just happened. What was the first cause of that? And what then led the first cell to magically progress to all of life? Instead, my leap of faith is to believe that God created the wondrous universe, that man was created in God's image, and that God's love was expressed in his son, Jesus. I realize that some Christians would believe my views are heretical, but I am convinced that we have engaged in arguments with science that are unnecessary and that can harm rather than deepen our faith.

And so my studies at YDS continued to enrich me as my professors shared their insights and knowledge. For instance, I profited from Professor James Gustafson's lectures in two classes, Christian Ethics and Sociology of Religion. Once when discussing the ethics of one's relationships with institutions, he recognized the necessity of some loyalty to institutions but cautioned us about absolute loyalty to any institution. He simply said, "Ride loose in the saddle." I have had occasion to remember that sage advice.

In my senior year, I enrolled in American Religious History, taught by Sydney Ahlstrom. Ahlstrom was a leading scholar in this field, having written a definitive textbook on American religious history. I remember him well. Professor Ahlstrom was a short, charismatic man with a burr haircut who lectured from a seated position. He had extensive knowledge, excellent insight, and a good sense of humor. I had always loved church history, and in my high school and college days, I had found American history fascinating. Ahlstrom's class convinced me that American religious history would be my field of expertise in religion.

I proposed to Ahlstrom that I do a special project on the division between Churches of Christ and the Disciples of Christ. I would carefully research the causes of this split by reviewing original sources, such as the leading periodicals of the era. I would also review the principal arguments made by leading ministers at the time.

I knew that the stated cause of this split was the use of instrumental music in worship and the existence of the missionary society. The Church of Christ believed that neither of these practices was scriptural, while the Disciples disagreed. However, my research proved the issues to be more complex than that. My study revealed that there were also sociological and sectional factors involved. There was a rural-urban divide in the nineteenth century; often the richer urban churches had organs, while the poorer rural churches did not. Additionally, the missionary society was more connected to northern churches. One of the northern churches' prominent members was James Garfield, a Union general and later president of the United States. Most of the opposition to the missionary society came from southern churches. I am suggesting not that the doctrinal issues were not important but that some cultural issues between the North and South, and between urban and rural areas, made the division more likely. I also wondered why it wasn't possible for one church to have instrumental music and another a cappella singing and still be in fellowship with each other. Unity does not require unanimity. I completed 101 pages of research and conclusions on the causes of this division. Ahlstrom was pleased with my work, and I was awarded six units of credit for this project.

I often reflect that when I arrived in New Haven in 1957, I was a disciple of Churches of Christ. When I left in 1962, I was a disciple of Jesus. At least, I tried to be. In his book *The Road Less Traveled*, Scott Peck writes that the map of one's life often changes. A map that served you well in childhood may need to be modified in adulthood as different circumstances and new truths arise. In my case, the map of my life altered in New Haven. The fundamental truths were still there, but the process of careful thought and study had led to me rethinking some of my previously held views.

Given the rethinking of my previous views, how would I proceed in the future? For instance, did I seriously consider leaving Churches of

Christ? No. I believed that I could still preach and teach within Churches of Christ because of their congregational autonomy. This meant that no central organization could rule over local churches. And I believed that some of our colleges, where I intended to teach, would allow more freedom than most local congregations.

Admittedly, I intended to be a voice for reform rather than merely following the party line. In its zeal to restore the form of New Testament Christianity, Churches of Christ had not sufficiently emphasized the spirit of Jesus, as taught in the Sermon on the Mount. We had even divided on minor issues, like whether Sunday schools were scriptural or how orphanages could be supported. I am reminded of Jesus rebuking the Pharisees, saying, "For you tithe mint and dill and cummin, and have neglected the weightier matters of the law, justice and mercy and faith" (Matt. 23:23). I was convinced that I could emphasize the essentials of the gospel rather than minor details. Furthermore, I felt that if I joined another church, I would simply trade the problems of my church for their problems. I knew our problems intimately; I could serve there more effectively than in any other place. An imperfect man would work in an imperfect institution. But I would no longer pridefully view my church as "the true church." I knew I could learn much from Christians in other churches. I would leave it up to God to determine who were members of his kingdom. It was not mine to decide.

Finally, on a less doctrinal note, I realized that Churches of Christ was where my heart was. This church was my family. It was the home of my father and mother; it was the home of my closest friends. There were many good people in this church, and I had spent my life as one of them.

I completed my studies at YDS and received my master of divinity degree in May 1962. All undergraduates and graduates of the graduate schools met on the main campus of Yale for the graduation ceremony. The featured speaker was President John Kennedy, who received an honorary degree. I remember his comment that now he had the best of both worlds: "A Harvard education and a Yale degree." After Kennedy's speech, we YDS graduates retired to the campus of the Divinity School, where I received my diploma. My parents honored me by traveling to New Haven for the occasion. While there, Lacreta and I took them into New York City to view many sites. We visited the Bronx Zoo and went on a boat ride around Manhattan.

Although church and education were certainly important, my life in the New Haven area remained focused on my family. Living apart from relatives gave Lacreta and me a certain independence and perhaps a clearer identity and bonding. We were a team. While I was the visible presence in the church, Lacreta was equally involved in the growth and nurturing of the congregation. She was also a safe sounding board and contributor as I shared the questions and issues I encountered in my education at YDS. We were both on a spiritual journey, and we were on it together.

Though I freely acknowledge that Lacreta bore the brunt of our children's care, I loved being a father. We watched Sharon and Sheila grow and eventually begin school. And on April 13, 1960, Amy Patricia Scott was added to our family. During those years in New Haven, I was the only male in a household of four beautiful women. We have family memories of going on picnics, playing in the snow, taking the children to the Bronx Zoo in New York City, and just the daily interaction of home life. Sharon and Sheila still laughingly recall the time we bowed our heads for the prayer at the evening meal, and I began it with "Hello." I suppose I had spent considerable time on the phone that day!

We kept in contact with our roots by making an annual trip to Texas to visit our parents. Of course, they delighted in their grandchildren, and at both parents' homes, our siblings and their families would come to visit. One memorable but less joyous incident occurred when we decided to drive to Texas for Christmas in 1960. We had driven all night to save money and time. Outside of St. Louis, it was snowing, and the road was slick. Lacreta had replaced me in driving. Suddenly, she lost control of the car, and we landed upside down in a deep ditch beside the road. I could hear baby Amy crying as I crawled into the back seat of the overturned car. Fortunately, aside from some bruises, no one was seriously injured.

The car was totaled, so the rest of the trip to Texas was by train. After our visit and celebration of Christmas at both parents' homes, we purchased a used car in Texas and made our way back to Connecticut.

Of course, living in New England was a different and rich experience for me and Lacreta. We sampled new cuisine, such as Italian food, and developed new tastes, such as lobster. We made trips to New York City, where we saw Broadway plays, visited the Metropolitan Museum, and toured iconic sites like the Statue of Liberty and Ellis Island. We subscribed to the daily edition of the *New York Times*; reading it daily broadened our knowledge of both our nation and the world. Our favorite movie house was the Lincoln Theater, which featured foreign films. We developed a taste for Ingmar Bergman films such as *The Seventh Seal* and *Wild Strawberries*.

Another highlight of these years was our friendship with Gary and Betty Freeman. We would visit them in Groton on a regular basis, or they would visit us in New Haven. We had come to Connecticut at the same time, and now we could share our experiences at the two small churches where we ministered. Gary and I would also share our theological thoughts, since we were going through similar experiences. And the adults would frequently splurge and eat at a restaurant. Gary and I would often finish an evening with a game of Scrabble; both of us were good players and quite competitive. It was mainly fun and a lighthearted break from our church work and studies.

Our time in New Haven was fruitful and fulfilling, but Lacreta and I both knew it would be coming to an end. As I was drawing near completion of my master of divinity degree, I began to explore the possibility of teaching at one of the colleges connected to Churches of Christ. My first choice was ACC because it was my alma mater, and I had worked there after college. And of course, it was near our parents. However, this was not to be. ACC had recently passed a regulation that no faculty member who was a close relative of a member of the board of trustees could be hired. This was enacted to avoid nepotism. Since my uncle, Crutcher Scott, was secretary of the ACC Board of Trustees, ACC was ruled out.

So I considered other possibilities. Fortunately, I had a contact: Dr. Norvel Young. Dr. Young had left Texas to become president of Pepperdine College in Los Angeles in 1957. He had known me at ACC and believed I was a young man of promise. So he kept in touch with me by occasionally dropping me a note asking me to consider coming to Pepperdine. Now I followed up on that possibility and indicated my interest in being on the faculty at Pepperdine. An interview was scheduled in New York City with Dr. Young and Bill Teague, vice president of the college. An offer followed that interview for me to become an assistant professor of religion at Pepperdine, beginning in the fall semester of 1962. I was also fortunate to receive a similar offer from Oklahoma Christian College in Edmond, Oklahoma. Lacreta and I gave careful thought to these possibilities, and we decided to go to Pepperdine.

Naturally, we had some regret in leaving New Haven. We had close friends in the church, and we had grown to enjoy our life in Connecticut. Those five years had proved life-changing, and I continue to look back at that time with fondness. However, I had a strong desire to teach at a college, particularly in the area of religion. Now we had that opportunity.

So in August, we packed all our belongings into a large rented trailer and began our cross-country trek of three thousand miles to Los Angeles. It was actually an action of some faith, since we had never visited the Pepperdine campus, and we had only been to Los Angeles briefly in 1956. At first, Sharon and Sheila were not enthusiastic about the move, since they had spent most of their lives in Connecticut. However, Lacreta and I sold them on California by telling them about Disneyland and the beach. Little did they know that they would spend most of their lives in that state or that their two brothers would be born there. We didn't know it yet, but we were all on our way to our permanent home.

CHAPTER 5

A Time to Gain, A Time to Lose

(1962–1972)

Figure 5.1. Jack was named provost of Pepperdine, LA campus, 1971

Figure 5.2. Jack and family, Westchester, ca. 1963

Our family geography was changing once again. For most of our lives, Lacreta and I had lived in Texas, and it was our virtual center of gravity. We thought we would return to Texas eventually. But now we were moving across America, this time from the East Coast to the West Coast. On our long journey from New Haven to Los Angeles, we stopped in Texas to visit with our parents, Lacreta's in Terrell and mine in Throckmorton. At each place, our siblings and their families came to see us. As at all Scott family gatherings, we shared food, laughter, and conversation and played many games of dominoes. Our visits at both places were very pleasant, as the grandparents showered much attention on Sharon, Sheila, and Amy, as well as on us.

Leaving Texas, we traveled down the long desert roads of Arizona and New Mexico to the California border. We were delighted to finally reach the sign welcoming us to California. Our plans were to spend the last evening in Westmoreland, California, before driving to Los Angeles. But we sadly learned that we had arrived at the opening of dove hunting in the Westmoreland area, and no motel room was available. So with a car filled with a patient wife and three tired children, we decided to make it on to Indio for lodging. Then more misfortune befell us. About ten miles outside of Westmoreland, a tire on our trailer went flat. Since our car jack couldn't lift a loaded trailer to change the tire, we bumped slowly back to Westmoreland to purchase a tire and had it installed at a service station. We left town again, but I had driven only a short distance when the new tire went flat. It turned out that the real problem was that the spring on the trailer had broken, and the jagged edge of the spring had flattened both tires. Here we were: it was after midnight, no motel was available, and I would have to wait till morning to have the spring welded.

It was then that a Good Samaritan came to our rescue. An oilfield worker happened to be at the service station. Realizing our plight, he graciously invited our family to spend the night in his home. And then the next morning, his wife prepared breakfast for our family. This certainly gave us a good impression of California as we arrived in the state. I was able to get the trailer spring repaired the next morning, and we resumed our journey to Los Angeles. After more long hours on the road, we wearily arrived on the Pepperdine campus late that evening. I had agreed to be the resident assistant of the men's dormitory for our first year; in turn, the college would provide us with a furnished three-bedroom apartment in the dormitory. Fortunately, they had prepared the apartment for our arrival.

Thus began our life at Pepperdine College in September 1962. This was not the campus that the name "Pepperdine" evokes today. In 1962, Pepperdine was still located on the original campus built in 1937, not the later Malibu campus overlooking the ocean. At this time, Pepperdine was an urban campus, located in a largely Black neighborhood. Though Pepperdine was connected to Churches of Christ, many in the southern churches considered it religiously liberal. For instance, though all the religion teachers of Pepperdine were members of Churches of Christ, not all its other teachers were required to be. In other Church of Christ colleges such as Harding, Abilene Christian, and Lipscomb, all the faculty were required to be Church of Christ members. However, Pepperdine had strengthened its connection to Churches of Christ when it had changed its top administration in 1957. Norvel Young, minister of the Broadway Church of Christ in Lubbock, became the president, and J. P. Sanders, dean of Lipscomb College, became the dean of Pepperdine College. And steps were taken to connect it more closely to the California Churches of Christ through the Pepperdine Bible Lectureship, which was widely advertised and well attended. In most respects, Pepperdine was still modeled after its sister colleges; for instance, no dancing or alcohol was allowed on campus. All students were required to take religion classes, and there was daily chapel. It was a friendly place, and students often formed lifetime friendships.

For our family, those early years at Pepperdine were a happy and fulfilling time. I began my teaching career in the Religion Department by teaching classes such as Old Testament Survey and New Testament Survey. I naturally was excited to fulfill my dream to be a college religion professor. I also enjoyed making new friends with fellow faculty members from a variety of different departments. I found we had much in common. I would frequently have lunch with these new friends, and our families would socialize in the evening. Of course, these gatherings were marked by humor, storytelling, and spirited discussions of many topics.

Lacreta also settled in, making good friends with several faculty wives. During this year, Lacreta became pregnant, and our first son, Gregory, was born on September 15, 1963. By this time, one year of supervising the men's dormitory had been enough for me, so we rented a home on Seventy-Seventh Street in Los Angeles, two miles west of the campus.

Two years later, we moved with our four children to Seventy-Ninth Street, which bordered the south side of the campus. We were now in faculty housing, and in addition to the convenience of just walking across the street to go to work, we found our lives enriched in unexpected ways. Pepperdine owned seven homes on this one block; another home on the block had been purchased by the dean of students, Jennings Davis. The Pepperdine families on this block formed a close bond by living near one another. It was almost like a commune. Wives often babysat for one another; the faculty children often became close friends. Even romance blossomed. In 1971, our oldest daughter, Sharon, had her first date with Cary Mitchell, whose parents lived in a home on that block. Cary and Sharon would marry five years later.

Two couples on that block became great friends of Lacreta's and mine: Mont and Patsy Whitson and Jennings and Vera Davis. We even shared some holidays together. For example, our three families joined with one other couple, Jim and Kitty Atkinson, for Thanksgiving dinner in 1963. We then maintained this custom for over forty years. The seventeen children of these four families often formed close friendships; they felt more like cousins than casual friends. It was in this house that our last child, Adam, was born on September 23, 1966, completing our family.

We had left behind our families in Texas, not realizing we would find a family of another sort in Los Angeles.

Another advantage of our living on Seventy-Ninth Street was the opportunity for Lacreta to complete her college degree tuition-free. Lacreta had been an excellent student when I met her, but our marriage and subsequent childcare had interrupted her studies at Abilene Christian College (ACC). But now she could walk across the street and complete her bachelor's degree in English. Despite caring for five children and fulfilling the duties of a minister's and professor's wife, Lacreta not only persevered; she excelled, completing her bachelor's degree in 1969. I was very proud of Lacreta's achievement as she was finally able to complete her interrupted college education.

As time went on, we began to love the state of California more and more: its unmatched scenery and booming, although volatile, economy. And certainly, its year-round mild weather was an additional benefit. The weather enabled me to make exercise a lifelong habit. It began on the tennis court, where I spent many joyous afternoons playing with and against faculty colleagues. One year I joined with Bill Teague to win the doubles intramural championship on campus. I also took up jogging. These habits were not only enjoyable, but they have had a health benefit, as I remain in good health even after passing my ninetieth birthday.

I was awarded a Danforth Teachers Grant to study for my PhD in history at the Claremont Graduate School in 1966, a banner year for me. This competitive grant was given to fifty teachers throughout the nation to enable those college teachers who had a master's degree to study for the doctorate. It was a generous grant, paying the total cost of tuition plus $6,000 a year.

I enthusiastically embraced this new opportunity. Pepperdine granted me a two-year leave of absence and allowed us to continue in our home on Seventy-Ninth Street. At Claremont, I enjoyed and profited from the quality of the professors, the assigned readings, and the interaction with other graduate students in the seminars. I relished the discussions in class and the opportunity to immerse myself in intense study during those two years. One of my professors, Douglass Adair, specialized in the Revolutionary period in American history. Knowing my background in religious history, he suggested that I might like to focus on John Witherspoon, the only clergyman to sign the Declaration of Independence, for my PhD dissertation. Adair believed that Witherspoon's *Lectures on Moral Philosophy* was quite significant in shaping the religious and political thought of this era. Unfortunately, Professor Adair committed suicide just six weeks before my comprehensive exams. However, Professor John Niven stepped in to lead these exams, and I passed the comprehensive exams in the spring of 1968.

I then followed Adair's suggestion and began my research for the dissertation on Witherspoon. I studied material in several libraries. I even went to the Princeton University Library; Witherspoon had served as president of that college from 1768 to 1794. My completed dissertation was approved, and I was awarded the PhD degree in American history in May 1970. Afterward, I did some additional work on this dissertation, and *An Annotated Edition of Lectures on Moral Philosophy* by John Witherspoon was published as a book by the University of Delaware Press. Someone later asked my son-in-law Cary if he had read my book. He wryly replied, "No. I am waiting for the movie."

One significant part of my ten years at Pepperdine was that I also served as the minister of churches in the area. I had preached regularly since 1951, and I now enjoyed continuing in this role. During my first year, I was minister of the Southwest Church of Christ. I then became minister of the Westchester Church of Christ from 1963 to 1966. This was a suburban church of about two hundred members, located about ten miles west of Pepperdine College. Our children enjoyed their excellent Sunday school. Lacreta and I made friends in the church, and we enjoyed the experience of working with the Westchester church very much.

It was at this church that I had a great opportunity. In 1964, a member of the church decided to take a trip to the Holy Land with his wife and young son. He and some other members of the church decided that if I accompanied him on this trip, it would enrich my teaching of religion.

So they donated enough money to make this possible. Of course, I was thrilled with this opportunity. I then discovered that I could purchase an around-the-world ticket from Pan American Airlines for only $250 more than the trip to the Holy Land. I quickly purchased this ticket, since this would enable me to visit other countries rather cheaply. I then called my good friend Gary Freeman, who at that time was minister of the Cleveland Heights Church of Christ in Ohio, to see if he would like to join me on this adventure. After some thought, he decided to take this trip. So Gary and I set out from Los Angeles on this journey around the world in May 1964.

The countries we visited were Hong Kong (China was closed at this time), Thailand, India, Egypt, Lebanon, Syria, Jordan, Israel, Greece, Italy, and France. We saw many spectacular sites, such as the Taj Mahal in India, the pyramids in Egypt, the Parthenon in Athens, the Colosseum in Rome, and the Arc de Triomphe and the Louvre in Paris. Even eating the various foods was an international experience: to dine at a White Russian restaurant in Hong Kong, to eat the hottest food I had ever tasted in India, to savor the Middle Eastern cuisine in Jordan, to drink Chianti and eat delicious foods in Rome, and to eat escargot for the first time in Paris.

But of special interest to Gary and me was our visit to the biblical lands of Jordan and Israel. Imagine seeing the Sea of Galilee, standing by the Wailing Wall, or walking around Calvary. To actually see and experience the area where Jesus and the apostles had been two thousand years earlier was very powerful. Because of our biblical knowledge, Gary and I were able to ask relevant questions of the guides and give instructions on the sites we wanted to see. Occasionally, I was amused by the inaccuracies of some of the guides. One guide pointed to a small structure on the road between Jericho and Jerusalem and claimed it was the inn where the Good Samaritan left the man beaten by robbers. I chose not to correct him by clarifying that this was a parable of Jesus rather than an actual event.

Of course, there were many moments of humor and fun. When driving to the pyramids outside of Cairo, I was sitting in the front seat with the driver, and Gary was in the back seat with our three-hundred-pound guide. Just before the return trip, Gary whispered to me, "It's your turn to sit next to Jumbo."

It was also in Cairo that I rounded a corner and was suddenly confronted by a beggar who had a baboon on a chain. I thought it wise to donate to him rather than risk a confrontation with a baboon. When we were in Athens, we were pestered by men offering us the services of a prostitute. Finally, we replied to them in total gibberish. Suddenly, they thought we were not American. Not being able to understand our manufactured language, they left us alone. The whole experience of this trip deepened my understanding of other cultures and my desire for international travel.

I enjoyed my three years with the Westchester church, preaching and carrying out other ministerial duties. I was not unhappy at Westchester, and they were not unhappy with me. But in 1966, an opportunity presented itself that I had to consider. A few years earlier, the Crenshaw Church of Christ in Los Angeles had begun with the specific purpose of bringing White and Black Christians together. To illustrate the success of this integration, they had four elders: two Black and two White. This church now came to me and wanted me to be their minister. This was not an easy decision, as Lacreta and I weighed this opportunity. But given our commitment to racial unity, we decided to make the move.

We never regretted this decision. The next six years we spent with the Crenshaw church were exciting and fulfilling. I was often in the homes of African Americans, and they were in our home. During these years, I began to understand more fully the pain experienced by African Americans after years of racial discrimination. For instance, I was visiting in the home of Philip Moore when the conversation turned to the time his family had moved into a predominantly White neighborhood. I asked him what happened after that.

He replied, with a look of deep hurt, "They just all moved away." I could imagine how I might feel if people thought I wasn't good enough to live near them.

Helene Spencer, an accomplished teacher, told me how she sometimes was followed by clerks as she was shopping in stores. The assumption was that she might steal merchandise. I could relate many similar stories; these simply deepened my commitment to racial justice. In my last year at Crenshaw, we brought in an African American, Billy Curl, to be the co-minister with me. After I left, he became the full-time minister and served that church effectively for over thirty years. Today the Crenshaw Church of Christ is thriving and growing, requiring two Sunday morning services to accommodate the crowd.

This was the 1960s, the peak of the civil rights movement. We all watched televised events as African Americans were brutally attacked and jailed for their protests against segregation. Our family watched the stirring speech "I Have a Dream," by Martin Luther King Jr., given at a rally in Washington, DC. All this was particularly relevant, since Pepperdine was located in a predominantly Black neighborhood, and our student body was about 20 percent African American.

In 1966, our area was shocked by the outbreak of the Watts riots, which were only a mile or so east of the Pepperdine campus. The National Guard patrolled this entire area; they were a common sight at Pepperdine. Fortunately, the rioting and burning did not extend to our campus, but the fear caused by this event was long remembered.

As the crisis deepened, the Black students at Pepperdine began to express their concerns about racial matters. For instance, Pepperdine had no full-time African American faculty at this time. Some of us were sympathetic to the concerns of these Black students. My close friend Jennings Davis, the dean of students, brought African American speakers to the campus to initiate discussion on these matters. I remember initiating a religion course entitled "Modern Ethical Problems"; the three main topics I focused on were race, war, and sex.

But the explosive event that brought this issue front and center was the death of a young African American, Larry Kimmons, on the college campus on March 12, 1969. Larry and his friends from the neighborhood often played basketball in the college gym in the evening. That evening, they found the gym closed and began to leave. On their way out, they encountered the college security guard, Charles Lane, who checked and confirmed that the gym was locked and told them to leave. At this point, the stories diverge. Lane claimed Larry resisted his orders; Larry's four friends disagreed with this version. Lane retrieved a shotgun from his car and then fired this gun, killing Larry. Whatever the differing backstories, the reality was clear: an unarmed Black youth, age fifteen, had been killed by a White security guard at the Pepperdine campus.

The surrounding African American community was understandably incensed. They had experienced a long history of mistreatment by White authority. There were rumors of unrest. The Black Panthers visited the campus. Some students began to leave, fearful for their own safety. After the death of Larry Kimmons, the college was forced to close down for a week. Then the African American students at Pepperdine drew up a list of demands. Some of these concerns had troubled these students for some time. The list was rather long; in some instances, concessions were made. For example, the college hired an African American, Calvin Bowers, as dean of ethnic studies.

Lane was charged with manslaughter. At the trial, the charge was reduced to involuntary manslaughter, to which Lane pled no contest. Lane received a one-year suspended sentence and a $500 fine. This light sentence angered the Black community; I could understand their anger. However, one result of this event, although not publicly stated, was that it heightened the desire of the administration to seek a new location for the campus.

One complicating factor at this time was that Pepperdine had taken a decidedly Republican turn during Norvel Young's presidency. David Baird, in his excellent history of Pepperdine University, *Quest for Distinction*, sums up this trend well. He writes that Young and his administration "believed that Pepperdine's chances at future success traveled in direct proportion to how well the college represented the political and economic interests of the well-to-do business community." Pepperdine began sponsoring Freedom Forum seminars and positioned itself as an alternative to the radical student movements of this period. A startling illustration of this rightward turn was an incident in May 1966. D. B. Lewis, a member of the Pepperdine president's advisory board and a supporter of the John Birch Society, died. His will left $1 million to Pepperdine.

However, the college could only receive this bequest if it granted an honorary degree to Dan Smoot, an ultraconservative radio commentator. This unusual bequest gained national attention. History professor Paul Randolph and I appeared on an NBC national news program denouncing the terms of the gift and urged Dr. Young to refuse the offer. Fortunately, Young eventually turned down the gift. However, I am sure the concerns about Pepperdine becoming too political that I and some other faculty publicly expressed did not endear us to the administration.

Meanwhile, the search for the possibility of a second campus site continued. On October 2, 1968, a gift of 138 acres of choice land in Malibu was given to Pepperdine University by the Adamson family. This land had a spectacular view: the Pacific Ocean bordered it on the south, and the Santa Monica Mountains bordered it on the north. This would be the location of a new Pepperdine campus. However, it was announced from the beginning that Pepperdine would maintain its campus in southwest Los Angeles as well. There were two reasons for that. First, it was uncertain that Pepperdine could raise enough money to move all its operations to Malibu. In fact, the idea was often expressed that the college at Malibu might be small, with an innovative and interdisciplinary curriculum. Second, hanging over this move was the accusation of "White flight" from a Black neighborhood. Pepperdine stated that it was committed to maintaining the urban campus at its original location. Unfortunately, later actions would confirm that the suspicion of White flight had been realistic.

Shortly after the gift of the land in Malibu, a committee was formed to create an innovative liberal arts curriculum for the Malibu campus. Bill Banowsky, executive vice president, and Pence Dacus, dean of continuing education, chaired the committee. Serving on the select committee were three administrators, Don Sime, Olaf Tegner, and J. C. Moore; and four faculty members, Jerry Hudson, Tom Dudley, Lloyd Frashier, and myself. I was a fan of an interdisciplinary curriculum, given my love of the humanities and my degrees in religion and history. This committee worked hard, read extensively, listened to faculty suggestions, and engaged in fruitful discussions. We ultimately recommended moving from traditional academic departments to four major divisions, which eventually expanded to eight. These interdisciplinary divisions were to emphasize the basic ideas that undergird human knowledge.

Later that year, I was given the title of dean. I then selected three faculty members to devise interdisciplinary courses in the humanities for the Malibu campus: Dr. James Wilburn, history; Dr. Grover Goyne, English; and Dr. Paul Watson, religion. All these excellent teachers had come to Pepperdine in recent years with doctorates in their respective fields from highly respected universities (Wilburn, University of California, Los Angeles; Goyne, Vanderbilt; and Watson, Yale). Their work was completed in the fall semester of 1970 and contributed effectively to the Malibu curriculum. Yet in the coming years, as Malibu became the main campus, the curriculum gradually became less innovative and more traditional.

I interrupted my administrative role, however, to spend the fall semester of 1970 teaching in Heidelberg, Germany, with Lacreta and our five children. A few years before this, Pepperdine had begun a Year-in-Europe program. They purchased a beautiful and spacious mansion in Heidelberg and outfitted it with lodging for students, classrooms for courses, and a nice apartment for a visiting professor. They also had a local director, Glenn Boyd, who had been a missionary in Germany and now lived in Heidelberg. I had earlier applied to teach in the program, and my turn came up in 1970. Although I now had administrative duties, I was given permission to teach that fall semester in the Year-in-Europe program.

It was a great opportunity for me and my family. Sharon and Sheila decided to take high school correspondence courses for that semester. Amy bravely enrolled in a German elementary school despite the language barrier. On the way to Heidelberg, the students and our family visited in London, Amsterdam, and Copenhagen. I recall that in Copenhagen, we were served breakfast that included cheese. Our three-year-old Adam took one whiff and said, "This cheese has bad breath." He was right!

Heidelberg itself was a delight. We could walk a short distance and visit the ancient and spectacular Heidelberg castle. Or we could walk or eat on the Hauptstrasse, the main street of Heidelberg. We could picnic near the beautiful Neckar River. In the fall, our family accompanied the students on a weeklong trip through Bavaria. The classes were arranged on Monday through Thursday, so the students could also travel during the weekends. We took advantage of this on separate weekends to visit places such as Paris and Switzerland; on other weekends, we often visited German cities. Lacreta got a break from cooking and household duties while we were there. We both felt refreshed when we arrived back in Los Angeles shortly before Christmas.

In early 1971, there was a dramatic change in the administration at Pepperdine. Bill Banowsky became the president, and Norvel Young was given the title of chancellor. Bill was a remarkable personality. It is understandable that he would become a college president. He was very charismatic: He could impress an audience with his superb speaking skills, and he could charm a prospective donor with his powerful personality. The fact that he was young and handsome didn't hurt. He was responsible for raising large sums of money for Pepperdine. Norvel Young had laid a strong foundation among rich Republican donors, yet it was Bill who generally closed the deal that funded the magnificent buildings on the Malibu campus. His charisma attracted donors like Blanche Seaver, a rich conservative widow, who would eventually give over $60 million to Pepperdine. (The undergraduate college at Pepperdine University is named Seaver College.) Bill was bold in making decisions. His intelligence and insight in understanding people were gifts that aided him in leading an institution.

Bill was someone I knew very well. He was a personal friend. He and I enjoyed long and candid conversations about religion, people, and ideas in general. He also significantly impacted my life professionally, appointing me to key committees and administrative positions. But he had reservations about my role at Pepperdine. Bill's main reservation about me was that I was not enthusiastic about Pepperdine's public embrace of Republican politics. So he decided I was better suited for the urban and diverse atmosphere of the Los Angeles campus. He called me into his office and said that he was designating me as the provost of the Los Angeles campus and Jerry Hudson as the provost of the Malibu campus.

Let me use Banowsky's own words to explain his reasoning. He writes about this decision in his book *The Malibu Miracle*. He compliments me on my understanding of African American culture and the inner city. But he also describes what he considers to be my Achilles' heel: "His moderately Democratic but deeply held convictions would not keep time with Pepperdine's Republican priorities. Jack had a lot of integrity. . . . Pepperdine's potential would demand doctrinal commitment in religion and politics. This meant both Churches of Christ and the Republican party."

Interestingly enough, I can understand Bill's reasoning to some degree. I was not the person who could attract wealthy Republican donors. After some reflection, I decided that becoming provost of the Los Angeles campus was a good opportunity. I would feel more at home at the urban campus. Admittedly, it would not have the splendor of the Malibu campus, but I felt the call to serve students of less privilege and more diversity. I realized I might have more freedom if I were geographically separated from the central administration. I also knew that the School of Business and the School of Education would probably need to stay in Los Angeles because of its central location.

My appointment had excellent support. The Pepperdine publication *Oasis* in 1970 makes the following observation: "The key to the Los Angeles campus is seen in the figure of provost Jack Scott. Scott commands the respect of nearly all segments of the university population, and is taking to his new job with a sense of Christian commitment at the same time realizing the tenuous and challenging nature of a church-oriented urban school."

I began to gather a team of administrators and faculty who shared my dedication to an urban campus. I successfully talked Grover Goyne, a close personal friend and an innovative thinker, into joining me. I knew that others, like Zane Reeves, Jennings Davis, and Don Sime, who were already on the Los Angeles campus, would be most helpful. And I was able to recruit African American teachers and staff who had the rapport and ability to relate to the surrounding community. I boldly titled my inaugural speech "A New Direction." I noted the challenges of an urban environment, but I also emphasized the call to Christian service. Our team then formed a select committee to revise the curriculum of the Los Angeles campus to make it more relevant to the student body. We were reasonably successful in obtaining some federal grants that were designed to assist the urban needs of inner-city America.

What I miscalculated, however, was the lack of real commitment of the college to the urban campus. The same article in the *Oasis* that praises my leadership raises this key question: "The commitment to the Los Angeles campus has always been questioned. How long will it be allowed to survive before the shop is closed and moved to the beachside campus? How much money will it receive in budget allocation?" Although trustees and top administrators publicly avowed their commitment to support the Los Angeles campus, I knew that some were secretly expressing the need to get out of Los Angeles as soon as possible.

I began to read the handwriting on the wall when the Pepperdine administration moved twenty-five thousand books from the Los Angeles campus library to Malibu. I continued to request greater financial support for the Los Angeles campus. Finally, on September 9, 1972, I wrote a four-page letter to President Banowsky and Chancellor Young, expressing my deep concern and documenting evidence of the failure to support the Los Angeles campus. I stated that I would find it difficult to continue if this situation did not change. I never received an adequate answer to this letter. The fact is that Pepperdine did eventually desert the Los Angeles campus when they sold it to the Crenshaw Christian Center in 1981.

Now I was faced with a decision. I could continue at Pepperdine. Yet I sensed that if I did, I would simply be a caretaker of the Los Angeles campus as it slowly declined. I could then go to the Malibu campus as either a professor or an administrator; after all, I was a full professor and had tenure. As a professor, I would not have to worry about politics. Yet as an administrator, I could not rise to the higher ranks because of my political views. And frankly, being a minority voice expressing opposing views to little avail did not appeal to me. I have always enjoyed throwing myself completely into causes in which I fully believed.

So slowly I began to realize that I would leave Pepperdine. Lacreta and I spent many hours discussing this painful decision. We had many close friends there. And since my graduation from college in 1954, I had always been employed by a church or a college that was connected to Churches of Christ. I had earlier pictured myself continuing that employment connection throughout my career. I knew that leaving Pepperdine would bring an end to that.

Despite the challenges, Pepperdine enriched my life in many ways, and I am grateful for my time there. I recall so many blessings during this ten-year period. Pepperdine offered me my original position on the faculty and gave me an administrative opportunity. I was able to earn my PhD degree while at Pepperdine. Yet perhaps the greatest gift I received from my Pepperdine experience was a painful one. I learned a lesson in humility. Prior to this time, my life had largely been a series of successes. I had topped off my career at ACC by being elected president of the student body. At New Haven, the church had tripled in membership, and we had built a new church building. I had successfully finished my PhD in 1970. I am not suggesting that I believed I had done all this without the assistance of others. I knew I had received immeasurable support from my parents, Lacreta, my teachers, and many other people. I thanked God for the way he had blessed my life. Still, my self-confidence had naively led me to believe that hard work, intelligence, and perseverance would probably lead to success. So I had tackled the job of provost of the Los Angeles campus with the help of others, believing that we would be successful in creating the campus I envisioned. I now realized that wouldn't happen. I am sure I made some mistakes, but it became clear that the administration at the university did not share my commitment. Sometimes we learn more from our defeats than our victories. One practical lesson I learned was this: before accepting any future opportunity, it is wise to carefully check out the environment to determine if success is reasonably possible. I was properly chastened; my skills, hard work, and determination did not guarantee success. I emerged from this experience a wiser and more humble man.

CHAPTER 6

A TIME TO CHANGE, A TIME TO LEAD

(1973–1987)

Figure 6.1. Jack and Lacreta, Orange County

Figure 6.2. Jack and Lacreta setting off on a bicycling trip, 1977

Much more quickly than I expected, an opportunity to make a move arose. My longtime friend Gary Freeman and his wife were visiting in our home. Gary, who was now on the English faculty at Orange Coast College, mentioned that their academic dean was leaving. I surprised him by saying that I might be interested in the job. After some thought, I decided to call the president of Orange Coast College, Dr. Robert Moore. I asked to meet with him to discuss the possibility of applying for the position of dean of instruction. We had good rapport in our long conversation, and he encouraged me to apply.

After applying for the job, I was interviewed by a faculty committee, by Dr. Moore, and by Dr. Norman Watson, chancellor of the Coast Community College District. I was then offered the position. Now "the rubber met the road." I had only a brief time to decide whether to stay at Pepperdine or make the move to Orange Coast. Moving represented a huge professional and psychological shift for me. After a lengthy and agonizing discussion with Lacreta about the decision, we finally decided to say yes to the offer. I agreed to begin as dean of instruction at Orange Coast College on January 1, 1973.

My shift from private Christian higher education to the public community college system seemed like an unlikely choice. I had neither attended a community college nor taught in one. But in many ways, it was an excellent fit. The community colleges of California are the largest system of higher education in the nation, educating over 1.8 million students. Their values align with my own; their egalitarian nature appeals to me. Students from marginalized communities and low-income households often do not have the means or opportunity to attend a four-year college. Community colleges are often the way up for the disadvantaged. They charge no or inexpensive tuition and accept all high school graduates. These values aligned with my efforts to maintain a viable urban campus at Pepperdine, a dream I'd had to let go with regret. So although I agonized over this decision, I have not regretted it.

At the beginning of 1973, I arrived at Orange Coast College to assume my position as dean of instruction. Although Lacreta and I intended to move to Costa Mesa, we delayed this move until the summer to allow our children to finish their school year. So I commuted from our home in the Los Angeles area to Orange County for several months.

I will admit that at first, I felt lonely at Orange Coast. I really knew no one there except Gary Freeman. This was my first professional venture outside Churches of Christ. It is not easy to leave a comfortable nest. Sometimes I sat in my office and wondered, "What am I doing here?"

Fortunately, Dr. Moore helped offset my unease by warmly welcoming and patiently mentoring me. On three consecutive Friday evenings, he and his wife hosted key college administrators in their home to introduce Lacreta and me. And I soon warmed to my task as the chief academic administrator of the college. The ten department chairs, who reported to me, were seasoned administrators. All but one was older than me, and most had spent many years at the college. So I knew I had to be cautious in handing out directives. I spent a lot of time listening. I wanted to fully understand the culture of Orange Coast College.

Also, as in all administrative positions, problems had to be solved. Faculty came to my office to get acquainted and receive advice. A few presented me with long-held grievances, believing that the new dean might magically solve the problems. Later that spring, I particularly enjoyed interviewing applicants for new faculty positions. Orange Coast was a growing institution; we were hiring over twenty new faculty that spring. Bob Moore and I conducted the final interviews. I appreciated his listening to my comments and advice as he made his final decisions.

Slowly I was introduced to the world of community colleges. Every institution has its vocabulary, so both at the college and in meetings with other deans of colleges, I began to pick up the "lingo." The annual meeting of the chief academic officers of the California Community Colleges was particularly helpful in the exchange of ideas. After building up trust, I was able to institute some changes and improvements at the college.

By then I had learned that humor can generally enrich one's life in any setting. And so it happened one day during my stay at Orange Coast College. Edward Teller, the "father of the hydrogen bomb" and later professor at the University of California, Berkeley, was scheduled to speak at Orange Coast. He was speaking on behalf of the nuclear energy initiative that was on the ballot in California. I was asked to pick him up at the home where he was staying in Los Angeles. I was glad to do this, since it would give me the chance to meet the famous scientist.

When I arrived at the home, Dr. Teller engaged me in conversation. In the intensity of his discourse, he moved forward and accidentally stepped on my foot with his prosthetic foot. Not having any feeling in his foot, he was naturally unaware that he was stepping on me. He continued on my foot for several minutes. Though I was uncomfortable, I did not want to embarrass Dr. Teller by saying anything. This incident enabled me to later regale people with the tale of how the famous Dr. Teller had injured me!

During my five years at Orange Coast (1973–78), there were developments in our family as well. Lacreta decided to pursue a master's degree in English at California State University, Long Beach. After completing this degree, she decided to teach on a part-time basis at some nearby community colleges. Our oldest child, Sharon, enrolled in my alma mater, Abilene Christian College, in the fall of 1973. She and her fiancé, Cary (her first love, from our days on Seventy-Ninth Street), then transferred to Pepperdine in the spring semester of 1975. They were married in March of 1976 and then graduated from Pepperdine in December of that same year. Meanwhile, our second child, Sheila, had a successful stay at Costa Mesa High School, where she was elected as one of the cheerleaders in her first semester there. She graduated in 1974. She was in love with Rick Head, and Lacreta and I were afraid she would marry young. We wanted her to go to college before marrying. So we encouraged her to spend the fall semester of 1974 in Pepperdine's Year-in-Europe program. That did break up the romance for the time being, but love was not to be denied. She and Rick would marry over a decade later. After returning from Europe, Sheila attended Orange Coast College. She then transferred to Sarah Lawrence, a liberal arts college in Westchester County, New York, where she graduated with a bachelor's degree in English in 1979. Our youngest daughter, Amy, continued her education at Costa Mesa High School and graduated in 1977. We wanted Amy to go to college as well, but she was in love with Paul Schones, and they were married a few months after graduation. We were not happy with that decision, since they were both quite young. However, they have had a successful marriage of forty-five years, with four children.

Our two sons, Greg and Adam, went through elementary school, middle school, and high school in Costa Mesa. Greg graduated from Costa Mesa High School in 1980. He was very active in drama; Lacreta and I often attended the plays he was in. Adam, our youngest, was the athlete in the family, earning letters in football, swimming, and wrestling. The family kidded me; they warned family members not to sit next to me as I watched Adam's wrestling matches, because I would move so vigorously as I watched Adam struggle. Adam was the student body president at Costa Mesa High School and graduated in 1983.

Orange County offered us many great recreational opportunities in addition to the professional opportunity I had been given. I was introduced to racquetball there, which appealed to me because I could easily transfer my tennis skills to this sport. I would often spend my lunch hour on the outdoor racquetball courts at the college. I continued to love the sport and regularly played racquetball until my retirement forty years later.

Another recreational activity that Lacreta and I enthusiastically began was bicycling. Lacreta was the leader in this respect. After we moved to Costa Mesa, she took a bicycling course at Orange Coast. She then encouraged me to purchase a bicycle. Orange County, with its constant sunshine and beautiful biking trails, is a mecca for bicycling. Sometimes on a Saturday morning, we would bike on the Pacific Coast Highway fifteen miles to Laguna Beach, eat at our favorite breakfast place, and then return.

But we took a giant step in the summer of 1974 when we decided to tour by bicycle. We flew to San Francisco, biked out of the airport, and biked all the way back to Los Angeles. We saw beautiful sights as we biked along the ocean: seagulls, seals, surfers, piers, and natural wonders. Biking along the Big Sur coast was spectacular, although we were totally exhausted after that sixty-seven-mile day. On this trip, we stayed at some lovely places at night, such as Monterey, Solvang, and Santa Barbara. I had planned the trip by plotting farm-to-market roads and bicycle trails where possible. But still, on occasion, we would have to bike on the shoulders of major highways. On one occasion, when a car came very close to us, Lacreta laughed and said, "Well, I won't have to shave my left leg for a while." We usually ate at restaurants, but sometimes we would purchase food and have a picnic lunch. We stayed in motels, and after a day of biking, we could eat with abandon at dinner without gaining weight.

Obviously, we were hooked. Bicycling trips became a staple of our time in Orange County. These trips were always in the summer, when my professional duties were lighter. On ten separate trips, we biked in seven states besides California, as well as in Canada, Italy, and England. On our second trip, we biked south along the beautiful Oregon coast and then eastward, along the spectacular Columbia River Gorge. The next year we rode from Montreal to New Haven, Connecticut. One hot afternoon in Vermont, we found a secluded place on a nice stream, took off our clothes, and had a refreshing dip in the water.

In 1978, we decided to visit Sharon and Cary, who were then living in Vittorio Veneto, Italy. We left Greg and Adam with Sharon and Cary and then biked for two weeks through northern Italy. Our bike trip took us around three beautiful lakes at the foot of the Alps. One evening we biked into a small town that had a large old hotel. Despite the language barrier, we were treated with gracious hospitality. As we biked away the next morning, the people stood up from their breakfast tables to watch these crazy Americans depart. After our two-week bike trip, we then went with Cary, Sharon, and our two young sons to visit Venice, Florence, and Rome for two weeks.

Perhaps our most strenuous bike trip was the following year in Colorado. I attended a weeklong conference of community college presidents in Vail. Afterward, we set out for Aspen, then biked over Independence Pass, which is 12,095 feet high. This required the lowest gear on our bicycles; still we had to take a brief rest every thirty or forty-five minutes before pressing on. We then visited the historic town of Leadville, which has the highest elevation of any city in America. We later climbed over Rocky Mountain Pass, another mountain of twelve thousand feet in elevation, before biking into Denver and returning home. We found the mountain scenery spectacular.

The following years brought another trip down the California coast and a journey from Newport, Oregon, where Amy and her husband now lived, to San Francisco. This was a seven-hundred-mile trip. The next year we flew to Great Britain, where we visited London and Edinburgh before beginning our bike trip. We biked first to England's Lake Country, where we visited the homes of William Wordsworth and Samuel Coleridge. This was thrilling to Lacreta as an English professor. We then biked south to see Stonehenge, Winchester Cathedral, and the beautiful English countryside. But on these trips, we inevitably experienced some tough days. The last day of our English trip was one of those days. As we biked back to London to fly home, it rained all day long. We arrived at the airport with our clothing and saddlebags soaking wet. Our last long-distance trip was in Wisconsin, where we visited Amish country. It was interesting to see the Amish buggies on the roads and watch Amish men plowing their fields behind horses or mules. And we also enjoyed biking along the magnificent Mississippi River.

These biking trips provided more than leisure time and exercise. We got a much closer look at nature than is possible in a car. Once when we were approaching Cambria, California, we stopped to see over one hundred pelicans diving into the ocean to feed on a school of fish. On a trip through the California redwoods, we rode within a few feet of some of those magnificent trees. The trips also expanded our knowledge of other ways of life. We met interesting people on these trips. Once, we struck up a conversation in a small café with an older couple who worked on a dairy farm. They became so excited about describing their work that they went out to their car to show us photos of their Holstein cows. On another occasion, I had a blowout in an Italian village, and a number of villagers gathered around to witness me changing the tire. Then one of the women invited us into her home and gave us a beer to refresh us. It was an astonishing education for a man who had started as a boy in a small Texas town. The trips also had a profound impact on our health and may help account for our longevity. We continued taking biking trips until health issues prevented Lacreta from continuing, but I was able to continue biking until well into my early eighties.

Although Churches of Christ were no longer my professional home, we formed church ties with the Costa Mesa Church of Christ, where we attended for two years. However, we began to feel uncomfortable with their legalistic approach. For instance, I was teaching a class composed of high school and college-age students when I was asked to preach at the Sierra Madre Church of Christ one Sunday. This church had rotating preachers, and I preached there on a monthly basis. It was a rather open church, and I enjoyed the monthly preparation and preaching. I told the Costa Mesa church I would have Lacreta teach my youth class that Sunday in my absence. I was quickly informed that would not be possible. Since women were not to "have dominion over men," and baptized young men were in the class, only men could teach the class. On another occasion, I sat through a class in which the errors of Seventh-day Adventism were exposed. Frankly, I received little spiritual nourishment from that discourse. I had tired of listening to what was wrong with other churches.

Then one Sunday, Lacreta attended another nearby church, Fairview Community Church. She was struck by the depth of the sermon and the general atmosphere of the church. When I later attended with her, I was similarly attracted, and so we became members. The church was connected to the American Baptist denomination, so we were familiar with their practice of adult baptism by immersion. We liked the fact that women could speak and lead worship. Also, there were meaningful and thoughtful discussions. It was a place where ideas could be expressed by sharp and insightful people without someone being accused of heresy. On a few occasions, I preached there in the absence of the minister, and Lacreta taught a women's class that was well attended. We also made friends, including close friendships with Gary Barmore, their minister, and his wife, Marti. We continued as members of this church until we moved from Costa Mesa to Pasadena. During this time, Lacreta and I still considered ourselves members of Churches of Christ and maintained our close ties with family and friends from that church.

I was happy at Orange Coast. I enjoyed the day-to-day challenges and the mentorship of Bob Moore. I was particularly impressed with his human relations skills. I would accompany him on his campus tours and observe him as he warmly interacted with faculty and staff. But after five years at Orange Coast, I felt prepared for the top leadership role in a community college. So in 1978, I applied for the presidency of Cypress College and was offered the position.

I began as president of Cypress College on March 1, 1978. Cypress had an enrollment of about fifteen thousand students. The buildings were attractive; they had been carefully coordinated from the beginning of the college. One advantage was that we did not have to move, since my commute from our house in Costa Mesa to Cypress College was only twenty-five minutes. This also meant our sons, who were still at home, did not have to change schools.

I would spend nine years as president of Cypress College. In my second year, there was an opening for the vice president of instruction position. I was able to bring my close friend Grover Goyne from Pepperdine to this position. Grover was highly intelligent and hardworking and possessed excellent judgment. But more than that, he was my confidant. We were almost always on the same page. We shared the same sense of humor, which made problem-solving more enjoyable and fruitful. We normally attended the national conference of the community colleges together in places like New Orleans; Washington, DC; and Orlando. We both liked to jog for exercise, and on a few occasions, we ran in 10K events together. Since we were both at ease in public speaking, we often presided at the opening faculty meeting with humor-laced information.

Only three months after I began as president of Cypress College, the state of California passed Proposition 13. Prop 13 had a great impact on the community colleges because it sharply lowered the property taxes in the state, reducing the funding for all public schools, colleges, and universities. As college president, I was charged with the challenging task of reducing programs and, potentially, personnel. I was able to avoid laying off any faculty or staff, but we slowly began to make other reductions. In the spring of 1979, I recommended that we no longer have a football team, which would save $90,000. Football has little effect on student enrollment at community colleges, since all the students are commuters, and many are part-time students. Furthermore, the Cypress program was unsuccessful; we had won only one of ten games the previous season. Fortunately, the president of the academic senate supported this decision. If cuts had to be made, most of the faculty preferred to cut football rather than make cuts to the academic programs. However, football is the holy grail to some fans and some ex-athletes. After a long and heated discussion at the board of trustees meeting, the board narrowly passed my recommendation by a 4–3 vote.

Another way that I addressed the funding problem was to strengthen the College Foundation. At the time of my arrival, the foundation raised some money for scholarships, but not a large sum. I knew there was potential for additional donations if alumni, friends of the college, and neighboring businesses were contacted. I began to add some key members to the board and was more aggressive in soliciting donations. I also realized that we needed an executive director, so we hired an experienced fundraiser, John Wagner. John and I realized that the Americana event, held annually at the college, had the potential to be a fundraiser. We moved it off campus, chose to honor a person from each of the seven cities in the Cypress College area, and sold tickets to the event. This event now nets an average of $120,000 annually for the college. We also began a swap meet, to be conducted each Sunday in the spacious parking lots fronting the college. The income from this event also contributes more than $100,000 to the college each year. Most community colleges are not aggressive in seeking donations, but I strongly believe that this can be the source of additional contributions for colleges and also raise the visibility of colleges in their communities.

Overall, we made progress at Cypress. Supported by three excellent vice presidents, I was more and more comfortable with my CEO role. Part of my charge was dealing with occasional disciplinary problems among the staff and faculty. For instance, the bookstore manager had an alcohol problem. After several warnings, I had to dismiss him when he was absent during the first week of school, the busiest time for the college bookstore. He was the only person whom I fired who ever thanked me for it. Several months later, he came to my office and said that this dismissal had led him to Alcoholics Anonymous and the road to recovery.

On another occasion, an instructor lost his temper and slammed material around the division office, frightening some of the female staff. I called him to my office and suggested that his behavior was unprofessional.

He replied sarcastically, “Exactly what is unprofessional?”

In turn, I said, “What you did was unprofessional, and if you repeat it, there will be serious consequences.” Of course, I didn’t spell out what those consequences might be. But he left my office sufficiently chastened, and I didn’t have to deal with him again.

Fortunately, it has been my experience that despite an occasional malcontent, the vast majority of faculty are dedicated and enjoy their work. It was essential for me as president to maintain their goodwill by listening to and encouraging them in the excellent job they were doing with students. The people skills I had developed over the years proved invaluable in my administrative role. It has been my observation that most college presidents who lose their jobs do so not because of a lack of competence but mainly as a result of poor human relations. One of the things I learned was that if the people you supervise like you, they will forgive quite a lot, but if they don’t like you, they will forgive nothing.

During my years at Cypress, I was once again fortunate to have the opportunity to travel. I learned of a program of six-week trips to underdeveloped countries for community college faculty and administrators that was sponsored by the University of Southern California (USC). These summer trips were underwritten by the US Department of Education. The only expense incurred by the participants was the tuition for six graduate units at USC; in return, each participant was to write an extensive report on a chosen topic from the nation visited. The format was to spend three weeks at a university listening to professors and experts from the country, then spend three weeks traveling throughout the country.

My first experience in the program was in the summer of 1982 in the West African nation of Nigeria. I spent the first three weeks at the University of Ibadan; luckily, all the lecturers were fluent in English. While I was there, I and two other teachers in the group took a trip to a small village. Our guide was a university student who was originally from that village. At the end of this interesting tour, I was unexpectedly presented with a live rooster as a gift. Over the years, I had been given many plaques and other gifts after a speech or visit, but never a rooster. I politely refused the gift. First, what would I do with a rooster? More importantly, these poor villagers needed every possession they owned. In the last three weeks of my time there, we toured different sections of Nigeria, marked by different tribes and different religions. The whole experience was fascinating. I wrote a report about education in Nigeria. I now read stories about Nigeria, the most populous nation in Africa, with much more interest and understanding.

My next experience was in China in 1984. I recall traveling from the airport to the center of Shanghai. I had seen crowds before, but I had never seen the massive crowd that was typical of this city. This was before the industrialization of China that typifies today. At this time, there were very few cars but thousands of bicycles. We spent the first three weeks at the University of Shandong in northern China. And then we traveled. I had the opportunity to walk on the Great Wall, the massive structure that was built two centuries before Christ.

We also traveled to the forbidden city of Beijing, where emperors once ruled, and the bustling markets of Guangzhou (formerly known as Canton). I was greatly impressed by this ancient culture, so much older than my own. In the years since that visit, there has been striking modernization in China. A few years ago, Lacreta and I were once again in Shanghai. The transformation is amazing: shopping malls, highways filled with cars, and the kind of dazzling lights you would see in New York City.

While my professional career was flourishing during these years, significant events continued in my family life. By that time, my parents had lived in Throckmorton, a small West Texas town, for twenty-two years. Here my father served as the minister for the local Church of Christ. He had served as an elder in the church in Sweetwater, but he boldly decided to be a full-time minister late in life. In some ways, my father became the pastor for the whole town, often preaching funerals for those who were not members of Churches of Christ. My father was very gregarious; he genuinely loved people. He regularly greeted and talked to people as he walked the streets of this small town. My mother was a full partner in this ministry: typing up his sermons, often going with him when visiting the sick, and teaching women's Bible classes. Personally, I believe that this period was the most fulfilling time in my parents' lives.

Both of my parents passed away during my time at Cypress. On August 5, 1981, I received a phone call from Throckmorton telling me that my father had experienced a serious heart attack. I immediately booked a flight to Texas. I arrived that afternoon; however, while I was traveling, he had suffered a second heart attack. This one was fatal. My father's funeral was held in the high school gymnasium, since the church was not large enough for the crowd. One small boy, upon hearing of my father's death, said simply, "Brother Scott loved me."

Sadly, my mother's life was deeply affected by my father's passing. Her first words to me after his death were "My life is over." However, she held up bravely for five more years, until her death in 1986. My parents lived rich and fulfilling lives. At their deaths, my father was eighty-four and my mother eighty-eight. Their deaths affected me deeply. It was a time of grief but also a time of meditation and gratitude for the love and basic values my parents had given me.

In my own family, things were also changing. Our children were thriving. In 1979, my daughter Sharon moved with her husband, Cary, to Lexington, Kentucky, to do graduate work at the University of Kentucky. Cary received his PhD in clinical psychology at Lexington, and Sharon her MA degree in anthropology. They then moved back to the Los Angeles area, where eventually, Cary would become a professor of psychology at Pepperdine, and Sharon would work part-time as a research assistant at the University of California, Los Angeles. My older son, Greg, attended and graduated from Pepperdine in 1985 and received his teaching certificate a year later. In his senior year, Greg was elected homecoming king, much as my father had been elected "Most Popular" while he was in college. On June 23, 1985, shortly after Greg graduated from Pepperdine, my second daughter, Sheila, was married to Rick Head. At that time, Rick was working as a machinist, and Sheila was working at United Cerebral Palsy. Soon Sheila began her work as a schoolteacher and would continue in this profession until her retirement. Our youngest daughter, Amy, who had married right out of high school, was happily married and living in Oregon. By this time, her husband, Paul, had developed a thriving fishing business. He began fishing in Alaska and eventually owned two large boats that fished in that area. Amy was the supportive wife and often the single parent, as Paul could be away for months as he fished in Alaska.

During this period, Lacreta and I were also blessed with the birth of five grandchildren. Three boys were born to Paul and Amy: Paul Jr. in 1978, Scott in 1979, and Tyler in 1983. In turn, Cary and Sharon had two girls: Nicole in 1980 and Sarah in 1986. These children brought much joy to our family. Each summer, our whole family would get together—children, sons-in-law, and grandchildren. Often we would rent a houseboat on a northern California lake and spend a great deal of time with water sports, such as swimming and water skiing. These were occasions of great fun, conversations, and love.

Another significant family event occurred in September 1984. Lacreta was offered a full-time position on the English faculty at Cerritos College in Norwalk. She had taught there on a part-time basis for several years, and when an opening occurred, she was hired. Thus began a wonderful teaching career of twenty years for Lacreta. She was very successful, eventually becoming the chair of the English Department. She often commented that she had two careers: first, as a wife and mother, and second, as a college English teacher. Her caring personality created strong ties with her many students.

My years at Cypress were happy years, both personally and professionally. But in 1986, an interesting opportunity arose in the North Orange Coast Community College District. The chancellor, Dr. Leadie Clark, was fired, thereby leaving a vacancy in this position. This position answered directly to the board of trustees and oversaw two colleges, Cypress College and Fullerton College. Many people encouraged me to apply. I did apply, since I knew I was well respected in the district. The two finalists were myself and Jim Kellerman, an administrator at the district. Dr. Kellerman was selected by a 4–3 vote. I admit I was disappointed. It was another difficult lesson for me.

However, I congratulated Kellerman and offered my support. One lesson I had learned over the years was that no one appreciates a sore loser. Furthermore, in retrospect, I became very thankful that I did not get that position. The opportunity that I received the following year would prove to be another significant turning point. I was about to embark on some of the most rewarding—and agonizing—years of my life.

CHAPTER 7

A Time to Build, A Time to Mourn

(1987–1995)

Figure 7.1. Photo of Adam, 1993

Figure 7.2. Jack and Lacreta took this photo in Altadena, using it with a Christmas card in 1990

In early 1987, I was contacted by Jim Tatum, a community college educator who had been employed by Pasadena City College (PCC) to assist them in their presidential search. He indicated that several people had mentioned my name as an excellent possibility for that position. He also informed me that the college had conducted an earlier search but had decided to go out again after reviewing the applicants. This increased my interest, since it indicated that there was probably not a strong internal candidate. Otherwise, the trustees would have selected that person in their initial search.

Moreover, I knew that PCC was a highly respected college and that Pasadena was a desirable place to live. But before applying, I called John Casey, the retiring president of the college, and asked to meet with him personally. I respected John and knew that he would give me straight answers. The two central questions I asked were these: Are the trustees capable and supportive? And what is the fiscal condition of the college? John gave me positive answers to both of these questions and provided me with further valuable information about PCC. So after careful consideration and discussion with Lacreta, I submitted my application.

Viewed as a strong candidate, I was interviewed by a representative committee composed of faculty, staff, and community members. I then was interviewed by the board of trustees. It was determined that I was one of the three finalists. A select group from PCC made a visit to Cypress College to ask how well I had performed there in my presidency. They received a positive response. In April, I got a call from the board of trustees. They had met and decided to offer me the position. I was excited to accept, and we met to finalize the contract. The contract was for three years and began on August 1. This was a decision I never regretted, for I can truly say it proved life-changing.

At the opening faculty and staff meeting in the fall of 1987, I shared my enthusiasm at being their new president and indicated how we could work together at PCC. In that first year, I determined that one priority would be to spend a great deal of time listening and getting acquainted. For instance, during the first week, I went in the evening to talk to the janitors when they reported for work. I told them how important their work was and how much it was appreciated. In return, they commented that this was the first time they had met with the college president. I recalled my father's wise advice years ago when I had first enrolled in Abilene Christian College. He had advised me to make friends with the janitor, for one never knew when one would need a friend. I also visited with each academic department. I began by briefly sharing my vision for the future, but I spent most of the time answering their questions and listening to their comments. Building trust is essential to good leadership.

Furthermore, I knew that I had to understand the culture of the college before I could institute changes. Bill Goldmann, an administrative dean, was particularly helpful in this respect. He had a long history at the college, both as a faculty member and as an administrator. So he would share his insights confidentially about the people and history of the college. Often before sending out a memo, I would share it with Bill to see if I had stated something that could be wrongly interpreted.

I believe that the strength of a college is basically the strength of its personnel. A college is a people's business, so the people who staff a college are key. A leader needs to review the present personnel, determine their strengths and weaknesses, and properly arrange the organization accordingly. So during that first year, I began to build an effective administrative team.

Sometimes reorganization was necessary to help personnel be more effective in their roles. I quickly realized that David Ledbetter, the vice president of instruction, had too many administrators reporting to him. So I took the very capable dean of student services, Ernestine Moore, and had her report directly to me. I also created a dean of academic services, who would oversee noncredit instruction, community services, and the radio station. This position would also report to me, and I chose Bill Goldmann for that job. These actions freed up David Ledbetter to do his main job, allowing him to focus on overseeing all the academic departments and tightening up class scheduling, which was badly needed. The changes benefited both the college and the respective administrators.

Not all challenges can be addressed through reorganization, however. Another key part of any college president's job is to solve problems. Harry Truman summed it up well with a sign on his desk that said, "The buck stops here." For example, when I arrived, I noticed that there was a problem in facilities. The campus was not as clean as it should be; trash and other physical matters were not handled well. I began calling in the facilities director to explain what I wanted done. But instead of a plan of action, he would give me a lengthy explanation as to why it couldn't be done. Finally, one day, I looked at him and said, "I don't want to hear about why it can't be done. I want you to tell me how you are going to get it done." The next week, he came into my office and announced that he had decided to retire. Mission accomplished! I then appointed a capable director of facilities.

In other cases, a president has to resolve entrenched department disputes. For example, early in my tenure, I had a parade of nursing instructors through my office complaining about the conditions in their department, with particular complaints about the department chair. Finally, I talked to the department chair and explained that I felt a change was necessary. She then began to explain to me how impossible the nursing instructors were.

At last, I said, "The reality is that the nursing instructors have tenure, and I certainly can't fire them all. However, I don't think you can be effective in the current situation." She resigned, and we replaced her with a strong woman who had been an army nurse. She had the iron hand within the velvet glove that made her effective as a department chair.

Sometimes the problems were small, as when mediating a dispute between faculty members. But sometimes a principle was at stake. For instance, the social science chair retired, and the department decided they wanted to select the new chair with no input from the president. This strategy was problematic because faculty sometimes want to decide what classes they will teach and what time they will teach them. However, schedules must meet the needs of students as well as those of faculty. So a department chair should be selected who will consider both student needs and faculty desires.

So I met with the department and tried to work out a compromise. They wouldn't budge in their demand, and I realized that if they had their way, that would set the precedent for the future selection of department chairs. Finally, they said they were going to appeal to the board of trustees. I said they had a right to do this; however, I felt the board would support me. I was correct. The board listened and then voted 7–0 against their proposal. As a result, a policy was established: The faculty of a department would have significant input in the choice of a department chair through interviews and recommendations. But the ultimate decision would be made by the president and the board of trustees.

Another part of my job as president was the often painful responsibility of firing or demoting administrators who were not effective in their positions. This needs to be done for the good of the institution but should be done with a gentle hand whenever possible. For instance, I soon realized that the dean of human resources needed to be replaced. The dean had been a dedicated and capable English instructor; however, she had been elevated to the HR position with no training in administrative issues. And a bad decision in personnel issues, such as dismissal, can be disastrous. So I kindly informed her of my decision to make a change but told her she could either return to teaching or retire; there did not need to be a public dismissal. She chose to retire, and I was then able to hire Jose Peralez, an experienced dean of human resources from another college.

Occasionally, serious disciplinary actions on my part were necessary. For instance, a staff member assaulted a supervisor. I called the staff member into the office and explained that it would be wise for him to resign. At first, he objected. But I explained that it was probable that he would be dismissed, and his resignation would be preferable to his dismissal. Fortunately, he agreed. On another occasion, I obtained the resignation of a male teacher who had made sexual advances to two different female teachers.

Fortunately, most personnel matters involved hiring or promoting someone rather than a dismissal or resignation. In my second year at the college, an important position opened up: the vice president of administrative services. This position oversaw all finance and facilities, which meant that most of the classified staff were overseen by this person. The opening for this position was advertised publicly, but I felt that I should do some searching privately. I called my good friend John McCuen, who had recently retired as president of Long Beach City College. I struck gold! He mentioned an administrator at Long Beach City College who might be interested: Jim Kossler. In praising Jim's work ethic, John said these memorable words: "He will get there before you do and leave after you do."

I called Jim Kossler immediately and encouraged him to meet with me to discuss this possibility. I was quickly impressed with his knowledge, intelligence, and grasp of the job. He applied for the position, sailed through the interviews, and was hired. Jim proved to be indispensable. When Jim was given an assignment, you could be sure he would complete it effectively and with dispatch. Furthermore, he and I had excellent rapport. We would meet regularly about the budget, which he oversaw masterfully. If we saw a problem in any department, such as overspending, we could address it quickly. His knowledge of construction was extensive, which proved invaluable when we subsequently undertook a large building program. The respect he gained at the college was evident when he was selected to succeed me as president in 1995. Jim and I remain close friends to this day.

Most of the time, my days were marked by pleasant encounters. I enjoyed talking to individual faculty and staff, occasionally visiting a class, and attending college events such as athletic games, plays, or musical concerts. Occasionally, I would be in the pastoral role of a counselor, such as when a nursing instructor came in to inform me that she had been diagnosed with multiple sclerosis. I comforted her and assured her we would make an accommodation for her disability. Frankly, it is a great privilege to work on a college campus where classes are being taught by dedicated teachers, enabling students to fulfill their potential.

The highlight of the school year at any college is graduation, but it has special meaning in a community college. Many of the graduates are the first in their families to go to college. It is joyous to see students march across the stage to receive their diplomas with hundreds of parents and spouses in the audience, cheering, as their special students are awarded. Some of those graduates are themselves parents who were brave to enroll and succeed in college while working to support their families. Some of the cheering crowd are children of those students.

At PCC, we would often choose an alumnus to be the graduation speaker. For instance, one year we had Joyce Kennard, an associate justice of the California Supreme Court, as the speaker. Born in Indonesia, she described how she and her mother had been imprisoned in a Japanese concentration camp during World War II. After the war was over, she then came to America. She had enrolled at PCC with little money but a great deal of determination. After finishing her associate's degree at PCC, she went on to the University of Southern California (USC) for her bachelor's and law degrees. She recalled fondly the contribution that PCC had given to her as a young immigrant woman.

My role as president also opened opportunities beyond the campus. Those years at PCC were a time when I became more involved in statewide activities in the California Community Colleges. I occasionally spoke or served on panels at conferences. I was active in the Association of California Community College Administration (ACCCA) and served as president of the organization for two years (1990–92). In 1993, the ACCCA honored me with the Harry Buttimer Award, given to two outstanding California Community College administrators every year. I also was appointed to the Regional Accrediting Commission of two-year colleges and served as chair of this organization from 1992 to 1994. This was a great professional development opportunity for me. We reviewed the accrediting reports of colleges, both public and private, in California and Hawaii. I also served on several accreditation visits to colleges. One amusing sidelight was an accreditation visit I chaired to the College of Mortuary Science in San Francisco. The name of the college president was Dale Sly, and the dean was Claude Grimm. Sounds like something out of a Dickens novel!

As time passed, I felt confident I had come to understand PCC well and had built up trust to initiate new programs. The most notable of these endeavors was an ambitious new building program. I had determined that perhaps the most pressing need of the college was the improvement of facilities. The campus was rather old, and certain facilities were clearly inadequate. In fact, no new building had been constructed at PCC for many years. I proposed to the board of trustees that the college employ an architectural firm to devise an overall master facilities plan. This firm would determine what new buildings should be built, where they should be located, what present buildings should be demolished, and what buildings should be remodeled. The board enthusiastically approved hiring such a firm, and $100,000 was allocated for this purpose. When the study was completed and the final plan approved by the board, I supervised the production of a color brochure that described the plan in detail. It included an artist's rendering of the new and remodeled buildings with their locations. It was labeled the "$100 Million Master Plan" because the needed funding totaled $100 million: $70 million in state funding, $20 million in college funding, and $10 million in private funding.

Of course, it is one thing to announce a plan. It is much more difficult to raise the funds, to oversee the construction, and to handle all the details, including the opposition that might arise. During my presidency at PCC, this project would occupy a large portion of my thoughts, time, and effort. But it proved to be one of the most exciting and fulfilling projects of my presidency.

The first project we undertook was to obtain state funding for a new library. Our library at the time was small and cramped; I was convinced that we could justify this need. However, I thought it wise to seek a consultant's advice on how to formulate a successful request to the state. I knew Cory Thompson, a retired vice chancellor of the Coast Community College District, who had vast experience in formulating building requests to the state. So he and I worked together to produce a construction plan for the new library with all the details, including location, total cost, and the possible purchase of some property. Fortunately, the plan for the library was approved and fully funded by the state.

But there was still work to be done for the library project to move forward. To facilitate the new construction, we wanted to close a small street that went through the east side of the campus. After some discussion, we negotiated a swap with the City of Pasadena. We could close this street, but we would give the city some property to allow it to widen Bonnie Street, which bordered the east end of the campus. With state funding, the college also purchased two businesses, a café and a transmission shop, which were razed, to ensure excellent frontage and parking for the library.

One other hitch occurred. The state legislative analyst argued that the state would be paying for additional parking, which was not a legitimate use of state funds. I argued that the college would not increase parking; it would simply move an existing parking lot to a different location. The decision would be made by a state assembly committee. I arranged to meet with Pat Nolan, the state assembly member who represented our district, to discuss the situation. He agreed with me. Fortunately, he was a member of the assembly committee that would make the decision. When the representative of the legislative analyst and I appeared before the assembly committee, the committee voted unanimously in favor of the college. I learned a valuable lesson: committee decisions are often made behind closed doors before a committee meets. This would be an invaluable lesson to me in my future political career.

The college broke ground for the new library in 1991, choosing to name the building after Walter Shatford, a revered member of the board of trustees. Upon completion, the library was dedicated in November 1993. It stands today as a beautiful building facing the most famous street in Pasadena, Colorado Boulevard, on the route of the annual Rose Parade. The project quickly proved its worth. In its first year of operation, the number of students patronizing the library doubled compared to the previous year.

The next project we tackled was a parking structure. Parking was a huge problem at the college. The PCC campus was only fifty-six acres, and expansion was almost impossible, since the surrounding area was mainly residential. Neighbors were constantly complaining that students often parked in front of their homes. The feasible solution would be to erect a multilevel structure, which could accommodate many cars but would take up a minimum of ground space. The structure would be located at the southwest corner of the campus and accommodate over two thousand cars. The cost of the structure was $10 million. This could be funded by a bond, which would be paid off by parking fees. However, legislation at this time limited the parking fee at community colleges to fifty cents daily. The college sought relief from Sacramento and was successful in getting the fee raised to one dollar per day. Thus the college was able to pay off the bond plus meet the costs of maintenance and security by the collection of the daily fees.

With the completion of the library and parking structure, the next project in the plan was a community skills center. Before I came to the college, the city had recognized the need for vocational training for jobs such as commercial sewing, electronic assembly, and grocery merchandising. The three entities involved—PCC, the City of Pasadena, and the Pasadena Unified School District—had combined to create a skills center. The school district provided a building that wasn't in use, and the college administered the project. It was the responsibility of PCC to provide the noncredit courses, hire the teachers, and collect funding from the state to finance the operation. However, the school district considered the use of the building to be temporary, so I knew that we needed to find a permanent location for this center. Since the center was serving a valuable instructional purpose, it was probable that the state would fund both the land and the building.

Fortunately, the mayor, John Crowley, called me and suggested that he knew of a property on Foothill Boulevard in Pasadena that might be ideal for the community skills center. On this land was property owned by the Pasadena Unified School District. A large fund from the state could reimburse the school district and provide PCC construction money for the community skills center.

However, as news of this possibility leaked, neighborhood opposition to the project soon arose. Two realtors led the charge, suggesting that the center would generate both excessive traffic and trash left behind by the students. I strongly suspected that the fact that a majority of these students were Black or Brown contributed to this opposition. We called a meeting of the neighborhood to discuss plans and answer questions. I vividly recall one angry man who, referring to the students of the community skills center, asked, "Who are these people?"

I replied, "These are the people who mow your lawns, who work on your homes, who live in your community."

We continued to meet with the neighborhood, but despite our making some concessions that would improve entrance and exit from the building, opposition remained strong. Some of these opponents even went to the Pasadena School Board to try to convince the district not to sell the property to the college. I had already met privately with Elbie Hickambottom, an African American who was the chair of the school board. He prized the value of the community skills center, and he listened to my suggestion that some of the opposition might be racially biased. As a result, he and the other board members quickly dismissed the complaint and moved forward with selling the land. The new center was completed and dedicated in 1995. The PCC Board of Trustees was kind enough to name the main meeting room in my and Lacreta's honor. And the faculty were thrilled to move from their borrowed building to a beautiful new building that continues to serve thousands of students today.

The next building project, a childcare center, was not part of the master plan. By that time, the college had hired my former colleague at Cypress College, Grover Goyne, to be the dean of advancement and executive director of the PCC Foundation. He and I met with a local foundation, the Berger Foundation, which had already given PCC $90,000 for computers for our Drafting Program. We had lunch with the trustees of the foundation and mentioned the need for a childcare center at the college. We had already learned that the wife of one of the trustees had a strong interest in childcare. We pointed out that such a center would serve a double purpose: it would serve as a center for those seeking a degree in early childhood education, and it would also be a source of childcare for the children of staff and students. The Berger Foundation promised to give the matter some thought. A few weeks later, we were surprised to learn that the Berger Foundation had purchased a piece of property across the street from the college and committed to providing funds to build the center. This generous gift totaled $3.8 million, and in 1995, the project was completed. It has served thousands of students and preschool children in the decades since then.

The final project in the $100 Million Master Plan was a new physical education and athletics facility. We knew that this facility would not be an easy sell. Community college athletics does not generate the popular support enjoyed by four-year colleges. One day, Jim Kossler and I were discussing ways to demonstrate the need for this facility when we hit upon the idea of declaring the present facility a health and safety hazard. This was not a spurious idea. The present facility, labeled the Men's Gym, was the oldest building on campus, having been built in the 1920s. It had no elevator to the second floor, which meant that physically disabled students had great difficulty accessing classes there. Furthermore, these students would be in grave danger in case of fire. We knew that if the state agreed that the facility was a health and safety hazard, its replacement would be given top priority. So we drew up a proposal with engineering proof of the inadequacy of the present structure.

Fortunately, this project was approved by the State Chancellor's Office and passed on for final approval by the state legislature. Once again, the legislative analyst objected, claiming we could simply remodel the old structure at 60 percent of the cost of a new structure. I went before the legislative committee and described in detail the inadequacy of the old structure, calling it "wretched."

To my relief, Senator Gary Hart, the chair of the Senate Education Committee, exclaimed, "Let's just get rid of that wretched old building!" The motion passed, and the athletics building was approved.

This building was not completed until after I left PCC. But during my tenure, the $100 Million Master Plan was approved and realized. It was a long journey, with much planning, countless meetings, many appearances before state committees, and some stiff opposition. Many people combined to make this plan successful: trustees, faculty, the College Foundation, friends of the college, and administrators. Yet it was worth all the effort. The Master Plan permanently changed the face of the campus with the construction of five new buildings. It also included the remodeling or refurbishment of some old structures. For instance, we had the three central buildings repainted. We also had a sculpture garden constructed in the middle of the campus with $1 million in private funding. Overall, it was wonderful to see a $100 million dream in 1988 become a reality in less than a decade.

I am proud of having shepherded the building plan to fruition during my years at PCC, but I am also proud of the increase in diversity in our faculty, administration, and staff during my tenure. Like so many community colleges in California, the majority of our student body was Latino, Asian, and African American. The overwhelming percentage of our employees, however, were White. Although the majority of our staff was White when I left in 1995, we had purposefully and markedly increased the percentage of our employees who were people of color. I had helped build a valuable legacy of another kind.

Family remained central in my life throughout my years at PCC. My marriage to Lacreta became richer and more rewarding with each year that passed, and the steady addition of grandchildren only added to our joy. Our daughters were established in happy marriages, economically stable and personally fulfilling. Our older son, Greg, would soon embark on a successful career and meet his beloved wife, Paula. Our younger son, Adam, had recently graduated from USC Law School with honors and begun a career at a prestigious Los Angeles law firm. Life was good for the Scott clan.

One feature that contributed to our family life was the purchase of a new home. When I first became president of PCC, Lacreta and I had been surprised at the high price of real estate in the Pasadena area. I commuted to work from our home in Orange County during my first year at PCC, but we continued to look for a home near the college. Finally, we found the ideal house in Altadena, a neighboring city just north of Pasadena. It was a spacious Tudor-style house located on a half acre of land. By then, Lacreta was teaching full-time at Cerritos College, where she very much enjoyed her interactions with students and her friendships with fellow teachers. (She also enjoyed her subsequent service as dean of liberal arts at Cerritos.) The drive from Pasadena to Cerritos was thirty-five miles with significant freeway traffic, but Lacreta agreed that living in the home we wanted was worth the long commute for her. The house would meet our family's needs, and it would also be a great place to entertain guests. We moved ahead with the purchase in December 1988, during my second year at PCC.

Our new home proved to be a wonderful place for our children and grandchildren to come. We had joyous gatherings on Christmas Eve, and our children and grandchildren frequently stayed with us. Some of our grandchildren even lived there with us for periods of our lives. That house became the heart of our family for the next twenty-three years.

We also found a second spiritual home at All Saints Church in Pasadena. We were struck by the insightful and powerful sermons of the rector, George Regas. Though we continued our association with the Church of Christ in Sierra Madre, where I preached regularly, we often attended All Saints Church and benefited from the classes, worship services, and George's sermons. On one occasion, Lacreta and I taught a class on successful aging.

The youngest of our children, our son Adam, had always been a sort of golden boy, blond and handsome, gifted with intelligence and more than his share of charm. From the time he was born, he had stood out as an inquisitive, intense child, filled with joy and vitality. He made it clear that he was not just the baby of the family. Despite his round cheeks and Gerber Baby cuteness, he was a force to be reckoned with. I can remember Adam, still in his high chair, listening intensely as his sisters Amy and Sheila argued a point. After a while, he interrupted, pointed out where each of them was right or wrong, and offered his opinion. It was not surprising that he grew up to become a lawyer. Adam was a standout in school from kindergarten on. I remember a neighbor telling me that when she went to register her daughter for school shortly after Adam finished kindergarten, she told the principal that the only person her little girl knew at the school was Adam Scott. The principal replied, "Well, Adam Scott is a good person to know."

In high school, Adam was a popular, academically excellent student. He also participated in athletics. Not greatly gifted, he nevertheless participated in sports with intensity and fierce determination. In his junior year, he was chosen captain of the wrestling team. He also won letters in football and swimming.

He went on to do undergraduate work at the University of California, Berkeley, which challenged him intellectually and spiritually and sharpened his already strong interest in social justice and the disenfranchised. Adam had always been a quester. He was deeply religious, but it was a faith he had explored, struggling through periods of doubt, moving from conservatism to a more ecumenical approach. I used to joke that Adam was the only one of my children who was more liberal than I had become. The "why" of things was as important to him as the "what." I remember when one of the female students was date-raped at a fraternity party while he was at Berkeley. Amid the anger and recriminations, Adam had a different reaction. He questioned *why* it had happened, what attitudes and beliefs were implicit in the fraternity system that made women vulnerable to assault.

Adam chose to go to law school because he wanted to be an advocate for those whose voices were often unheard or ignored: the homeless, victims of racism and sexism, gay men and women, and even displaced animals suffering from neglect. The two words that best describe Adam as a young man are *egalitarian* and *compassionate*. Adam lived his beliefs.

I remember him coming home one weekend covered in paint because he had spent the day painting an elderly woman's home in South Central LA. Adam was never a saint—he was irritatingly messy and sometimes used his charm to get his way—but he was as good a son as one could hope for. When Adam graduated from law school in the spring of 1993, he was hired by the prestigious Los Angeles law firm of Crosby, Heafy, Roach, and May. Lacreta and I looked forward with excited interest to what our younger son would achieve there. We were builders, and we were intensely proud of the family we had built together.

By the fall of 1993, by almost anyone's standards, Lacreta and I were living a charmed life. Our world was happy and secure. And then one day, in the twinkling of an eye, that world was shattered.

On October 23, 1993, Lacreta and I took a walk around the neighborhood with our infant granddaughter, Erin, in a stroller. Our oldest daughter, Sharon, and her two younger daughters, Sarah and Erin, had come to visit us. They had spent the previous evening in our home while Sharon's husband, Cary, and their oldest daughter, Nicole, were away on a Girl Scout camping trip. When Lacreta and I got back from our walk with the baby, I went to take a shower. Shortly before I emerged, there was a knock on the door.

Sharon answered the door and, to her surprise, was greeted by a deputy sheriff. As Sharon stood at the open door, he explained that he had come to give us some bad news. Our son Adam was dead. Struggling to speak, Sharon called her mother to the door, where the deputy repeated the horrific news.

Unable to fathom what she was hearing, Lacreta asked, "Was it an accident?"

The deputy replied, "No."

Then Lacreta asked, "Was he shot?" I don't know how she intuited this, but she did.

He replied, "Yes."

Moments later, I emerged from the bathroom and saw the deputy. I was given the unthinkable news.

Stunned as though by a physical blow, I collapsed to the floor, and Lacreta and I held each other as we sobbed.

How was this possible? Just the evening before, Adam and I had talked on the phone. He had told me, "Save a seat for me. I'll join you for church on Sunday." He then added as he closed the conversation, "I have to hang up. I'm leaving for a party." I had just talked to him. How could he be dead?

We struggled to understand as the deputy laid out the basic facts. Adam had gone to a party hosted by a young man named Ethan Dubrow. Ethan was a gun aficionado, having four guns in the house, three of which were loaded. He sat down on the couch next to Adam that night holding an "unloaded" shotgun. Some partygoers later said that Ethan made a teasing remark about Adam's opposition to guns. As Ethan rose from the couch, the powerful shotgun went off. The bullet went through Adam's jugular vein, killing him instantly. Police arrived shortly, and Ethan was temporarily jailed, but his father posted bail, and he was released.

A short time after the deputy sheriff departed, I called our other children—Sheila, Amy, and Greg—to inform them of Adam's death. Sheila and Greg came over immediately. Unfortunately, Amy and her family were living in Hawaii at the time, so they could not arrive until the next day. Close friends came to comfort us as news of the tragedy spread. I still remember Kitty Atkinson, our dear friend from our years at Pepperdine, standing at the front door to greet people as our family huddled in the bedroom, comforting one another. On the day of Adam's death, George Regas came to see us. During our time at All Saints Church, George had become a valued friend.

That day I looked at George and said, "How will I ever get over this?"

And George replied, "You won't. You will always limp. But you can go through life with a limp."

That blend of realism and hope was just what I needed.

Our children did everything they could to comfort me and their mother. Even though they were also in deep mourning, they constantly showed their care for Lacreta and me. Our older son, Greg, even moved into our house temporarily and would often sleep in the same room with us in case one of us was in distress during the night.

In the midst of our overwhelming grief, there were many difficult things that had to be done. We had to choose a funeral home, select a gravesite, and then plan a funeral. We chose the Mountain View Cemetery to lay Adam to rest, an older cemetery in Altadena near our home. I recall walking with my close friend Jennings Davis, another of our "extended family" from our Pepperdine days, to choose the gravesite. I told Jennings that I had always assumed Adam would one day be choosing my gravesite rather than my having to choose his. And at the viewing before the funeral, I wept before the body in the coffin, confirming without a doubt that it was Adam who was dead.

The funeral was held at All Saints Church. This beautiful, historic old church, which seats one thousand people, was filled to capacity. Adam had made such an impression in his brief tenure at the law firm that they closed their offices for several hours so that the firm lawyers could attend the funeral. Family members and friends from every walk of our lives crowded together to honor our son. The service was personal and deeply moving. Jennings Davis gave the eulogy. I particularly remember one thoughtful sentence: "God, too, is angry at Adam's death." Then Greg told the story of Adam's birth from his point of view. At three years old, Greg had spent his days surrounded by females: his three older sisters and his mother. He longed for another male, so he did the logical thing. He asked God for a brother. With the faith of a child, he had no doubt he would receive one. When Lacreta gathered the children a short while later to tell them she was expecting another baby, Greg immediately asserted, "Oh, I know. It's my brother." He told a tearful audience that day that he had always considered Adam his baby brother and closest friend. Adam was the special brother God had sent him in answer to prayer. As Greg sat back down in the pew next to his brother's coffin, he unconsciously reached over and patted the coffin where his brother now lay.

Many of Adam's friends gave testimonials. They often mentioned his love for the homeless and his rescue of animals that needed a home. They gave example after example—some poignant, some humorous—of Adam's impact on their lives. One friend described Adam as embodying "the church whose doors never closed so that all who found the way could nurture their souls." After the funeral, we proceeded to the graveside for the burial. At the conclusion of the graveside service, some of Adam's male friends lingered at the grave. As the workers began to shovel the dirt to cover Adam's coffin, his friends asked for the honor of shoveling the dirt to bury their friend.

And they did.

At this time, I often read from 2 Samuel 18:33, where King David mourns the death of his son, echoing David's agonized cry: "O my son Ab'salom, my son, my son Ab'salom! Would I had died instead of you, O Ab'salom, my son, my son!" It was true. I would gladly have died in Adam's place. After all, I was sixty at this time; Adam's life had been extinguished at age twenty-seven.

How do you recover from a blow like Adam's loss? Lacreta later said, "You don't recover, but you have to continue." In the months ahead, I had many occasions to remember what George Regas had told me. I had to keep going, even if I limped. In one respect, I was incredibly blessed. I had Lacreta. We had always shared conversations, so we could freely talk about Adam and the unbelievable pain of his loss. We both limped after Adam's passing, but we were always there to hold each other up. It was the halt leading the lame, but we did not fall into a ditch. We had shared decades of joy. It prepared us, when the time came, to share our grief.

CHAPTER 8

A Time to Make Friends, A Time to Speak

(1994–2008)

Figure 8.1. Jack's senate victory party, 2000

Figure 8.2. Governor Arnold Schwarzenegger signing Jack's Bill

Following Adam's funeral, Lacreta and I faced the most difficult task, the grieving process. For some months, my first thought upon awakening each morning was "Adam is dead." No more would he burst through the backdoor with a cheerful greeting! No more would he and I have lengthy philosophical and political conversations! No longer could I envision the long and meaningful career he would have!

Lacreta and I sought grief counseling with an able therapist, Dr. Larry Schulte. We also met for some time with a special group that had also lost children to violence. I sought out books to read on the subject, such as *Why Bad Things Happen to Good People*, by Harold Kushner. Kushner had lost a son to progeria, a genetic disease that causes children to age prematurely and die. I also found most helpful *Lament for a Son*, by the theologian Nicholas Wolterstorff, who lost his son in a mountain climbing accident. Lacreta made the decision to step down as dean at Cerritos and return to the classroom as a full-time instructor, a less stressful and more fulfilling role that allowed her to work directly with young people.

Friends were invaluable. Fellow administrators temporarily took on extra responsibilities to ease the transition when I returned to work at the college. A close friend, John McCuen, who was serving as interim president at Porterville College, came to PCC and spent an entire day with me. Lacreta and I also received an outpouring of letters from people who recounted how much Adam had meant to them. He is fondly remembered even now. Last year, I attended the meeting of the board of directors of a statewide higher education program, California Competes. Also on this board was Libby Schaaf, mayor of Oakland. I looked at her and thought she must be the same age Adam would be. It turned out that she and Adam had served as interns together at a law firm in Oakland. When I identified myself as Adam's father, she rushed over and hugged me. Obviously, she remembered the tragic circumstances of his death. She recalled how outstanding Adam had been and remembered his strong impact on his fellow interns.

A painful aftermath of this event was the trial of Ethan Dubrow. His careless handling of a loaded gun resulted in his being charged with involuntary manslaughter. His family had the means to provide him with the best legal defense, including Robert Shapiro, who defended O. J. Simpson at his criminal trial. Lacreta and I attended the trial, and I testified. Eventually, Ethan was found guilty and given a four-year probated sentence. We struggled with what seemed like a light sentence for taking our son's life. For some time, I found it difficult to say the words of the Lord's Prayer that enjoin us to forgive those who trespass against us. But years later, Ethan and his wife came to our house to ask for our forgiveness. He promised that he would no longer have any guns in his home. Lacreta and I told him that we forgave him; we hold no ill will against him. Harboring bitterness hurts the one who holds the resentment far more than the person who is the target. Letting go of that resentment has been an ongoing process for our whole family.

A positive outcome of Adam's death was the creation of a fellowship at the University of Southern California (USC) Law School. Dana Treister, a close friend of Adam and a fellow student at the law school, came to us with the idea. We decided to create a fellowship that would fund summer internships for law students at USC. In applying for these internships, students would be required to spend their time with organizations that specifically support social causes.

We knew this would be exactly what Adam would have wanted. Applicants would have to provide a letter from the organization they would be working with and the reason this issue was important to them.

After a personal interview with the leading applicants, the committee can choose one or two applicants to be funded that year. The selection committee is composed of Dana; myself; Adam's brother, Greg; Nicole Rodger, Adam's niece and an attorney; Scott Altman, a professor who taught Adam; and the two recipients who were awarded the fellowship the previous year.

The donations for this fellowship exceeded our expectations. Today the endowment for this fund is $440,000. We never touch the principal, but we can still spend a portion of the interest to select two applicants each year in perpetuity. Between 1995 and 2020, we awarded fellowships to thirty-eight recipients. Some of the causes that these students have chosen are domestic violence, immigration, the disabled, fair housing, children who need representation, consumer protection, and racial and sexual discrimination. We have received many letters from recipients who have been enriched and have accomplished a great deal during the summer fellowship. Many have decided to devote their legal careers to social causes after their graduation.

In early 1995, an interesting offer was presented to me. Pepperdine University offered me the opportunity to be a Distinguished Professor of Education. I was intrigued. I thought it would be interesting to share my knowledge and experience with graduate students. Most of these students were already in education; they believed a doctorate in education would improve their skills and better their chances for advancement. I knew that I could be particularly helpful to those working in community colleges. I also realized that having reached my sixty-second year, teaching would be less demanding than administration.

Whether to leave the community college system was not an easy decision, since I had thoroughly enjoyed my years as president of Pasadena City College (PCC). I knew that the board of trustees at the college did not want me to leave, nor did the faculty or administration. Of course, I knew that sometimes it is wiser to leave when they want you to stay than to stay when they want you to leave. When I discussed it with Lacreta, she said she simply wanted me to do what *I* wanted to do. Fortunately, if I decided to leave PCC, my decision would not affect the location of our home or her work as a faculty member at Cerritos College.

As I considered the offer, I looked back on my years at PCC. I felt that it was a better place than it had been when I arrived. The foundation of the college was much better. We had added effective members to the foundation board. PCC had raised about $10 million in private funding during my tenure. I had facilitated the completion of the $100 Million Master Plan. We had also instituted more effective class scheduling; more classes were offered in the afternoon and on the weekend. A solid administrative team had been built. I would be leaving the college in good condition, with leadership that would carry on effectively if I left. Finally, I decided to accept the Pepperdine offer. At the PCC Board of Trustees meeting on March 7, 1995, I announced my retirement from PCC. I agreed to continue as president until November 30. That would give the college sufficient time to select a new president before my departure.

But as Robert Burns, the Scottish poet, wrote, "The best laid plans of mice and men go oft astray." And so it was with me.

In September 1995, six months after I announced my retirement, my life took another unexpected turn. I was driving when the car phone rang. It was Jeanette Mann, a PCC trustee. She and I had become good friends during my eight years at PCC. She informed me that she; John Van de Kamp, former California attorney general; and Fred Register, a top political consultant, wanted to meet with me and discuss the possibility of my becoming a candidate for the California State Assembly.

This was a complete surprise to me. In fact, I was startled! I had never considered this possibility, nor had I discussed with anyone a desire to seek legislative office. I asked them what had led to this request to meet with me. I found out it had come from a meeting of a progressive committee in Pasadena called ACT. ACT was begun in the early 1970s to discuss political issues and, in some instances, to back candidates seeking local and statewide offices. Although successful in some local races, they had never been successful in backing Democratic candidates for the state assembly and state senate. However, they thought there was a real possibility the following year to defeat the Republican incumbent in the assembly, Bill Hoge, if they picked the right candidate.

As they discussed the matter, someone had suggested, "What we need is someone like Jack Scott."

And then someone else had added, "Why don't we ask Jack Scott?" They became excited about this possibility, so they chose Jeanette, John, and Fred to meet with me. They told me that they considered me a strong candidate for several reasons.

First, I had been successful as president of PCC, a role that gave me favorable visibility in the community. Furthermore, I had often spoken to groups throughout the community, and my speaking ability was a plus. Crucially, I had not taken any public positions on political issues, since as a college president, I had chosen to be nonpartisan. So I could be viewed as moderate. My friends knew that I was a registered Democrat and, thus, knew my political leanings, but I had kept them private during my years at PCC.

The fact that I had announced my retirement from PCC but had not yet taken up my role as professor at Pepperdine made me available. So Lacreta and I agreed to meet with the three of them one evening in my college office. They made the best possible case for several hours, even mentioning that they had made contact with the state Democratic Party before contacting me. The party had realized the strength of my candidacy and pledged their support. In this meeting, I asked them many questions about what would be involved if I agreed to be a candidate. I concluded the meeting by stating that if I had to give an answer that evening, the answer would be no. But I assured them that I would give the matter careful consideration and that I would let them know in a reasonable period of time.

I took several weeks to give careful thought to this matter. I had several hesitancies. I knew I would have to raise considerable money to contact the four hundred thousand people in the assembly district. I also knew that politics was a "contact sport"; that is, I would be harshly attacked. Furthermore, I had already promised Pepperdine University that I would accept their offer of Distinguished Professor of Education.

And I realized that the decision to run for this assembly seat would call for a radical change in my life. I might work hard night and day for the next twelve months and yet lose. If I won, I would be in the arena of public office, which I had never experienced. On the other hand, I could continue in the world of higher education, an area for which I had prepared and in which I already had thirty-five years of experience.

But the possibility of a seat in the state assembly had its allure. My father had been in politics. I had always had an interest in politics, and I realized that it did have the possibility of accomplishing a great deal of good. I might be able to accomplish some of the things I had dreamed of for Adam. I could take up where he had left off.

As Lacreta and I discussed the matter further one evening, she asked this penetrating question: "Jack, if they appointed you to that position, would you take it?" I had to admit that I would. However, I was still unsure about what to do. If Lacreta had preferred I not run for the assembly, I would have turned down the opportunity. But being the supportive wife she had always been, she was willing to back whatever decision I made.

I continued to give much thought to this matter and decided to consult confidentially with others. I talked to my children, and they all were positive about my running for office. I prayed about the matter and even went to Adam's grave to say a prayer. Of course, knowing Adam, I knew he would have said, "Dad, go for it." Adam believed strongly in political causes, particularly in those causes that supported the marginalized in society. He would have loved the campaign and would have engaged fully in it with his effort and advice. After all, I had pictured him in politics, not myself.

Richard Katz, the Democratic leader of the assembly, encouraged me to enter the race. He answered many questions and pledged support. But I wanted to hear from someone who would discourage me—a "devil's advocate." I had a good friend, Jim Young, who was chancellor of the Kern County Community College District in Bakersfield. Jim had run for the state senate a few years before. He was narrowly defeated and had experienced some very dirty tactics and false accusations in the last days of the campaign. I phoned Jim and was surprised to hear him encourage me to run. Jim felt that his run for political office had largely been a good experience, and he particularly emphasized how he had met many good and interesting people during the race. He also said that politics needed good and capable people like myself.

So I began to clearly lean toward running for the assembly. However, there remained one more hurdle. I had made a commitment to Pepperdine University, so I made an appointment to meet with David Davenport, president of Pepperdine. I explained my dilemma, but I also made it clear that I would keep my word to Pepperdine if the university so desired. David could not have been more gracious. He said that I now had an unusual opportunity, and he encouraged me to take it. Furthermore, he said I could teach in 1996 while running for office, and even if I were defeated, I would still have a permanent position on the faculty. So I privately informed the persons who had first approached me about running that I had decided to take the plunge.

I had a nice farewell reception at PCC prior to my retirement on November 30. There was some sadness on my part, since this had been the richest professional experience of my career. The board of trustees kindly complimented me and presented me with a proclamation at the last board meeting.

During the first week of December, I held a press conference at PCC, formally announcing my decision to be a candidate for the California State Assembly in 1996. Now the race was on, and the next twelve months would be both hectic and exciting.

I selected Fred Register as my campaign manager. I knew that having the right campaign manager was the first and most important step in conducting a successful campaign. Fred had conducted many campaigns. He knew the Pasadena area extremely well, and he and I had an excellent rapport. He would advise me at every turn in these intense twelve months. He would keep me encouraged, but he would also tell me unpleasant truths when I needed to hear them.

The next necessary step was to raise money. There was no way for me to compete in an area of over four hundred thousand people without having funds to get my message out. So I needed to get on the phone in the evenings and ask people directly to support my campaign.

Fred suggested I use two politically experienced women, Judy Boggs and Wendy Soltes, to assist me. They had a list of people who had previously contributed to Democratic campaigns. I would initiate these calls, explain to the prospective donor my reason for running for the office, answer any questions that the person might have, and ask for a specific contribution. Judy and Wendy would note the contribution promised and mail the letter to collect it. I was pleasantly surprised that no one seemed to resent the call, and the response was generally positive.

There were also some organizations that were supportive, such as labor unions, teacher organizations, and plaintiff attorneys. I would arrange to appear before these groups or contact their key leaders. I would also go to Sacramento and solicit donations. Of course, I had to prove that I was a viable candidate before contributions generally were made. In the assembly, only ten to fifteen of the eighty seats were close races. Most assembly seats were decidedly Republican or decidedly Democratic. Fortunately, I was a candidate who began to prove that I had a good chance of winning. By the end of the campaign, I had raised over $800,000, which matched the amount of money that my opponent had raised.

Other factors besides fundraising were important. One was a ground campaign: knocking on doors to discuss my qualifications and strengths with voters. To head up this ground campaign, we brought in a young man, Graham Foreman, who was experienced in this area. This campaign required careful planning. We selected areas of the district to target. Graham trained volunteers on exactly how to do this work and provided the party identifications of the homes to be visited. If no one was present when the volunteers visited the home, they left campaign literature for the occupant to read. We particularly gathered on Saturday mornings. Lacreta and I would often join the volunteers. This was a great experience. I really began to understand what the issues were.

There were also moments of humor. I recall one man asking me if I was going to be "a lawmaker."

I said, "Yes."

He quickly replied, "I want an un-lawmaker. We already have too many laws."

Another part of campaigning was mailers. Since television ads in the Los Angeles area were prohibitively expensive, our main method of communication had to be through the mail. My opponent, incumbent Republican Bill Hoge, was noted for his negative mailers. His first mailer accused me of having a racial quota system at PCC. He portrayed me looking across a desk at a White man and saying, "You are not hired." Although I had worked toward increasing ethnic diversity at the college, I'd never had a quota system. Additionally, Hoge never referred to me as PCC president; he labeled me simply as "a liberal professor."

In sharp contrast, Fred Register designed my mailers to be primarily positive, extolling my record at PCC and pointing to my leadership in education. The local newspaper, the *Pasadena Star-News*, endorsed me. They also commented negatively about Bill Hoge, particularly on his failure to serve his district. They compared Hoge to a rocky mountain goat; you know he is there, but you never see him. We reproduced that editorial in one of our mailers. I also gathered many other key endorsements that could be played up in my mailers.

Of course, I made as many public appearances as possible. I had made friends in the African American community while president of PCC, so I often spoke in African American churches.

But, of course, it all came down to Election Day in November 1996. We had an election party at the Hilton Hotel that evening where many of my supporters gathered, hoping for a victory. My brother, Morris, who had come out from his home in Phoenix to help in the last few days, was there, as well as my son Greg. When the first returns came in, Hoge had a lead. However, Fred encouraged me, saying these votes were absentee ballots and that Hoge's margin was less than the usual absentee vote for Republican candidates. Hoge's lead slowly narrowed, but I was still behind at one in the morning. I decided to head home, thinking that I might lose by a few hundred votes. Morris, Lacreta, and Greg accompanied me home. When I arrived, I asked Greg to call the election headquarters.

Greg reported that I had suddenly surged into the lead. I had a hard time believing this, so I had to call for myself. Each time I called, my lead increased. Finally, I won by a healthy margin of nine percentage points (53 percent to 44 percent).

The next morning, I was interviewed by the local newspaper and a few radio stations. Adam Schiff, the Democratic candidate for state senate, had also been elected. Until then, the Pasadena area had always been represented by Republicans for these two offices. So the following morning, the *Pasadena Star-News* had a picture of Adam and me standing together on the front page with the headline "There's a New Party in Town."

I, along with other Democratic victors, was flown to Sacramento to celebrate my victory. The assembly had now changed hands. Previously, the Republicans had control of the assembly by 41–39 votes. The recent election had changed four seats. Now the Democrats were in control, 43–37. Yet I was the only Democrat to defeat an incumbent. The other three Democratic gains had been in open seats, previously held by Republicans who had been termed out.

In early December, I was sworn in, in a ceremony in the assembly. Some of the campaign workers came to Sacramento to celebrate and attend the ceremony. But much had to be done before the actual beginning of the legislative session in January. I had to select a staff for both my Sacramento office and the district office. Once again, Fred aided me in this process. I asked Bill Goldmann, who had retired from PCC, to head up the district office. I found Scott Wetch, who had previously worked in legislative offices, to be my chief of staff and head up the capitol office. After some consultation with Cruz Bustamante, the newly selected speaker of the assembly, I was placed on certain committees and asked to chair the Budget Subcommittee on Education.

Of course, Lacreta and I also had to locate a place to live in Sacramento. We decided to rent an apartment near the capitol. Lacreta decided to teach the fall semester at Cerritos College but take a leave of absence in the spring semester to accompany me to Sacramento. In turn, I would be in Pasadena when the legislature was out of session from September through December. This plan would enable us to be together most of the year.

As I began to walk the stately halls of the capitol and settle into my office, I sometimes was amazed. I once said, "If someone had suggested earlier in my life that one day, I would be in the legislature in California, I would have laughed. I would have replied that I don't intend to move to California, and I don't intend to be a politician." But here I was, and the state capitol would become the center of my life for the next twelve years.

Frankly, I felt like a college freshman as I began my first year in the assembly. The first time I presented a bill to a committee, I simply returned to my seat after the presentation. Scott, my chief of staff, whispered to me that I should continue standing at the lectern so I could answer questions from members of the committee. All these protocols were new to me. However, as time progressed, I began to feel more and more comfortable. I began to learn the customs and language of the legislative body.

I soon fell into a consistent schedule as a legislator. On Monday and Thursday mornings, I attended the regular sessions of the assembly, where I was called upon to vote on the bills presented by assembly members. I also voted on bills that had been passed by the senate and sent over to the assembly for a vote. All these bills had been approved by the appropriate committees. In an annual session, I would vote on six hundred or more measures. To vote intelligently required me to study the bills. In this process, I was aided by my staff, the recommendations of organizations, and the caucus. I also attended meetings for the committees on which I served. My office hours included visits by fellow legislators, constituents, and lobbyists who desired to influence my vote.

Once I settled in, I began to introduce bills on a variety of subjects. For instance, the leaders of San Marino, a city in my district, were concerned about Water District plans to build a large water tank behind San Marino High School. Since an earthquake fault was beneath the proposed site, the citizens were concerned that an earthquake could unleash water that would flood the high school. I introduced a bill to stop this proposed construction. After considerable debate, I was able to get the bill through both the assembly and senate committees and then passed by the two houses. But there was still a possibility that the Republican governor, Pete Wilson, would veto the bill. San Marino was a wealthy and heavily Republican city. I suggested to the lobbyist that he get San Marino citizens who were Republican donors to contact the governor to encourage him to sign the bill. Success! Perhaps my experience navigating bureaucracies and working with college faculty had prepared me for life in the legislature.

Naturally, I was active in introducing bills on educational issues. I also served on both the Education and Higher Education Committees and discussed the bills that came before us. And I was often consulted about matters pertaining to the community colleges because of my years of experience.

I also led the way on bills related to gun control. I had begun speaking on this topic soon after Adam's death, and I continued to promote this cause in the legislature. I successfully authored a bill that required that every gun sold in California be accompanied by a trigger lock. The bill did not require that the lock be used, but this incentive resulted in many guns being safely stored. Another important bill I carried, sponsored by the California Police Chiefs, stated that someone carrying a concealed weapon without a permit could be charged with either a felony or a misdemeanor. Previously, they could only be charged with a misdemeanor. This measure resulted in many dangerous persons being incarcerated, particularly gang members. In my presentations on these gun bills, I would often relate the tragedy of Adam's death. I pointed out that Adam's assailant received a four-year probated sentence, but Adam received a death sentence. Naturally, my bills on this issue were strenuously opposed by the National Rifle Association. This organization would later spend considerable money to defeat me. Fortunately, they did not succeed.

Aside from my work at the capitol, I spent much time working in my district. Legislators normally flew home to their districts on Thursday afternoons and returned on Sunday afternoons. I would meet with the constituents in my district during this time to listen to their suggestions and concerns. This also gave me the opportunity to attend local events. It was important that the voters see me and know that I was involved. I was frequently asked to participate in parades. For instance, I always participated in the La Canada Memorial Day parade. Lacreta and I rode in an old classic car and waved to the crowds that lined the streets. I also regularly participated in the Montrose Christmas parade. On one occasion, the Glendale Fire Department provided me with a large fire truck. Some of my children and grandchildren rode with me and Lacreta in the parade. It was a joyous and exciting occasion for all of them. We had more opportunities to make contact with the district when the legislature was not in session (September to December). During the December holidays, we had an open house in our home that many people attended. I must add that Lacreta was a tremendous asset during my time in the legislature. She met people with ease and could skillfully carry on a conversation about almost any topic. Of course, we had been partners in all our varied endeavors, so her outstanding ability in the political arena was no surprise to me.

Since the term for the state assembly was two years, I was scheduled to run again in 1998. My Republican opponent was Ken LaCorte. He used my stand on gun control against me and received funding from several gun organizations. We engaged in a debate and each sent out several mailers before the election. I also conducted a door-to-door campaign, as I had in the first campaign. I believed my visibility in local events and my response to constituents during the previous two years were helpful. But I always approached election evening with some anxiety. One time I said, "There are two ways to run for election: scared and hard." Fortunately, I increased the margin of my previous victory from 9 percent to 16 percent, winning 65,652–46,652.

After my victory, I asked Antonio Villaraigosa, the speaker of the assembly, to appoint me the chair of the Insurance Committee. This appointment proved fortuitous. In 2000, our committee launched an investigation into some questionable activities by the state insurance commissioner, Chuck Quackenbush. Some large insurance companies had been fined, but Quackenbush had reduced these fines if they contributed to a charitable foundation controlled by his office. One questionable expenditure by this foundation was $3 million spent on television programs featuring Quackenbush giving insurance advice. It was suspected that this provided publicity for Quackenbush, who was often mentioned as a future candidate for governor.

As chair of the Insurance Committee, the assembly provided me with a seasoned attorney to sit next to me and advise me during the hearings. We began to uncover more transgressions as the hearings progressed. Two of Quackenbush's aides had used state credit cards to fatten their own wallets. They were later to serve prison terms for their misdeeds. Slowly, more and more corruption was uncovered, until even the Republican members of the committee turned against Quackenbush. He began to realize he would probably be impeached, so on July 10, 2000, he resigned. The entire process of the hearings, the revelation of the corruption, and Quackenbush's resignation were widely covered by the press and television. And the public reaction to our cleaning up corruption was very favorable. One humorous newspaper cartoon had me holding a large frying pan over a fire, with Quackenbush in the pan.

Engrossing as my legislative duties were, my heart remained first and foremost with my family. Many important events occurred during my years in the legislature. Our son Greg was married on May 15, 1999, to Paula Doty. He named his brother Adam as his best man in absentia. Six years later, Greg and Paula were blessed with the birth of a daughter, Kate, on September 29, 2005. In 2000, Sheila and Rick adopted a beautiful five-month-old baby girl from Fiji named Cecilia. She joined their two older twin brothers, both of whom were adopted. But the adoption of grandchildren into our family didn't stop there. After raising three sons, Amy and Paul were so touched by the plight of Ethiopian orphans that they traveled to an orphanage in Ethiopia. There they found a twelve-year-old girl named Alemay. She had been placed in the orphanage after the death of her parents. Alemay spoke no English and had been raised in an impoverished Ethiopian village. Amy and Paul took her home to Oregon, where they carefully nurtured her. Today Alemay is a high school graduate, speaks excellent English, and is engaged in studies beyond high school.

Another rich family event occurred in 2001. Our oldest grandchild, Paul Schones Jr., graduated from the University of Oregon and decided he wanted to enroll in a chiropractic college in Whittier, which was close to our home in Altadena. So we invited Paul; his wife, Christi; and their one-year-old daughter, Hailey, to live with us. Lacreta and I were away much of the year because of my service in the legislature in Sacramento, so it was no inconvenience to us. In fact, it was a great joy. Two years later, Paul and Christi blessed us with another great-granddaughter, Erika. As you can imagine, Lacreta and I became very attached to Paul and Christi and those two little girls. It was a very harmonious relationship; we greatly enjoyed one another's company. When Paul graduated and this young family returned to Oregon, I will admit that tears were running down my and Lacreta's cheeks as we watched them drive away.

There were other important family events during these years. Lacreta's parents passed away: Reta in 2003 and A. V. in 2005. Both were ninety-two years old at the time of their deaths and had lived rich, fulfilling lives. Also during these years, Lacreta and I were fortunate to celebrate our golden wedding anniversary on September 2, 2004. I reflected once again on how remarkably I'd been blessed in finding Lacreta.

We also traveled extensively during this period. We were close friends with Jon and Joan Jones, a couple from our college days. From 2001 to 2008, we traveled together with Jon and Joan on trips to seven different destinations: Spain, Bermuda, Honduras, Australia / New Zealand, eastern Europe, Italy, and Ireland. We always enjoyed one another's company. Our conversations were generally marked with humor, memories, and comments on the wonderful sights we were seeing. For example, we witnessed the religious parades during Passion Week in Spain; walked across the famous bridge in Sydney, Australia; saw the fantastic green countryside in Ireland; and visited Sicily, Naples, and Rome in Italy. Most of these visits were bus tours with knowledgeable guides, excellent meals, and fine lodging. It was always an interesting and educational experience to interact with people of other cultures. Lacreta and I thoroughly enjoyed traveling and doing it together. We were truly fortunate to have these experiences through the years.

Lacreta and I also purchased a timeshare condominium with Diamond Resorts in Kauai, Hawaii. We traveled there for a week in the summers. Kauai is a beautiful island, and our condo was on a beach facing the Pacific Ocean. We always invited relatives or friends to share the condo, since it had two bedrooms. Lacreta and I always found our stays relaxing and enjoyable.

In 2003, I received an unexpected honor. I was named Outstanding Alumnus of the Year at Abilene Christian University. I guess one never outgrows the desire to be honored by home folks. Many of my relatives and former classmates attended this event. Dr. Royce Money, president of the university, presented the award.

Back home, my service in the assembly continued to be marked by much activity. I introduced several more bills. Some of these bills were based on my personal experience. For example, as the grandparent of two adopted boys at the time, I became a voice for easing restrictions on and encouraging adoption. At that time, California law permitted biological parents to change their minds up to six months after an adoption. One can imagine the pain of adoptive parents who, after bonding with an adopted child, suddenly have this child taken away. My successful bill drastically shortened this time period.

I also successfully authored a bill containing safeguards against unscrupulous sales of annuities. The impetus was learning of Lacreta's ninety-year-old uncle being sold an annuity that he clearly didn't need. One item in the bill required the annuity salesperson to give the prospective customer a twenty-four-hour notice before attempting the sale. Both the adoption and annuity bills were opportunities for me to use my personal experience to serve the common good in my role as a legislator.

My life has often been marked by unexpected opportunities, and another such opportunity soon appeared. Adam Schiff, the state senator in my area, decided to run for Congress. Adam had been elected state senator in 1996, the same time I was elected to the state assembly. Since our districts overlapped, he and I had become good friends and often worked on projects together. But since Adam was running for Congress, he could not run for reelection to his state senate seat in 2000.

Many people encouraged me to run for Adam's vacant seat in the senate. There would be advantages to serving in the senate rather than the assembly. State law limited senate service to two terms. I could serve eight more years in the senate, whereas I had only two years remaining in the assembly because of the six-year term limit in that body. Furthermore, I was now an experienced legislator, and I believed that I could continue to serve effectively. However, I recognized that winning the senate seat was no slam dunk. There was another Democratic assembly member—Scott Wildman, on the other side of the district—who had announced his intention to run for the senate.

Once I also decided to run, he and I were forced to square off against each other in the Democratic primary. It was the first time I'd had an opponent in a primary. Since it was an intraparty contest, the state Democratic Party did not take sides. It was a heated contest. We each had a base in the senate district, and we often were seeking endorsements from the same people and organizations. Scott Wildman and I had a few debates. Both of us had a mailing campaign and a door-to-door campaign. Ultimately, I was able to win the primary, receiving 53 percent of the vote to 47 percent for Wildman. Of course, there remained the general election in November 2000. My Republican opponent in the general election was Paul Zee. Fortunately, I was able to increase my margin of victory from past elections. I received 158,145 votes to Zee's 100,901 votes (59 percent to 38 percent).

Lacreta and I now thought it probable we would be in Sacramento for another eight years. This proved to be a safe bet, since the Republicans chose not to run a candidate against me in my 2004 reelection campaign.

So we bought a nice three-bedroom home on Thirteenth and F Streets, just six blocks north of the capitol. This proved to be a great place to host family and friends.

I took the oath of office to become a state senator in December 2000. I was fortunate to remain in this office for the next eight years. During this period, I served under two senators who held the leadership position of senate pro tem: John Burton (2000–2004) and Don Perata (2004–8). I was able to establish a warm relationship with both of these senators. They were supportive and expressed their confidence by placing me in key positions.

Perhaps my greatest opportunity came in the field of education. I served as chair of the Budget Subcommittee on Education from 2002 to 2008. This was important because education represents one-half of the state budget. I also served as chair of the Education Committee from 2004 to 2008. This committee dealt with all policy issues in both higher education and K–12 education in California.

I authored a variety of education bills during my tenure, but three stand out. First, I was asked to create a new funding formula for the California Community Colleges (CCC). I drew up an outline of this funding and then brought together all the key players (CCC administration, trustees, and faculty) and urged them to reach a consensus. I did not want them quarreling among themselves. After many hours of discussion and some compromise, they hammered out a conclusion. I presented this funding formula to the legislature. It was passed by both houses, and the governor signed the bill that became law. The process was sometimes contentious, particularly because there was so much money involved. There is some truth in the hackneyed old saying "He who loves sausage and respects the law should watch neither one being made."

Subsequently, I was approached by Dr. Charles Reed, chancellor of California State University (CSU), to author a measure that would permit CSU to offer the doctor of education (EdD) degree. At that time, the University of California (UC) was the only public university in California that could offer a doctoral degree. There was a real need for this practical doctorate, particularly for those aspiring to be administrators in the public schools and community colleges. I and others had encouraged UC to meet this need, but they had simply dragged their feet. In consultation with Dr. Reed, I drew up a bill to allow CSU to offer this degree. UC quickly organized to oppose this bill and walked the halls of the legislature in opposition. I was able to get the bill passed in the senate, but the real battle remained in the assembly. Dr. Reed was invaluable in his support; he called the presidents of the twenty-three CSUs and encouraged them to contact their respective legislators to vote for the bill. Today, fourteen CSUs offer the EdD degree. At the beginning, this degree was granted to 53 graduates in 2010. But now this number has grown tremendously; in 2023, the EdD was granted to 271 graduates. In the past fourteen years, 2,996 graduates have received this degree from CSU. The completion rate is an impressive 92.5 percent. And over 60 percent of these graduates are students of color. It is always rewarding to realize that this legislation has had such outstanding results.

The third bill I want to highlight addressed a problem that forced me into a conflict with the major teachers' union in the state, the California Teachers Association (CTA). I had previously sided with the CTA on issues such as increased funding for public schools. But I discovered that some teachers' unions in the larger cities of the state had negotiated a clause in their contract with which I strongly disagreed. This clause forced schools that had advertised an opening to accept any teacher within that district who met the minimum qualifications and desired to fill that vacancy. In my view, this created a serious problem. For example, a principal of a struggling school might be trying to fill vacancies with young, energetic teachers who would tackle this challenge. But a teacher from another school in the district might show up and demand the job. Perhaps they were dissatisfied with their current assignment and wanted a change; however, they were not a good fit for the new opening. The principal was out of luck. They would have no choice but to fulfill the contract by hiring the transfer. The *Los Angeles Times* labeled this practice "the dance of the lemons," for too often it was the perennially dissatisfied "lemons" who applied for transfer.

Many warned me, even some newspapers that endorsed my bill, that I would lose in a contest with the politically powerful CTA. However, I talked with legislators of color and pointed out that it was their schools that were often saddled with incompetent teachers. Many of these legislators were aware of the problem. For instance, Fabian Núñez, speaker of the assembly, agreed with me. The bill passed the assembly despite the fact that Jackie Goldberg, chair of the Assembly Education Committee, opposed the bill, and the CTA lobbied heavily against it. As I have often observed, politics is a "contact sport." It also passed the senate and was enthusiastically signed into law by the Republican governor, Arnold Schwarzenegger, who complimented me for having the courage to carry this bill.

Of course, I did not author only bills on education. In my eight years in the senate, I also authored measures in areas such as health care, insurance, and gun control. And on some occasions, my bills were not successful. For instance, I authored a bill that would have authorized community colleges to offer classes in state prisons. I believed that these classes would give prisoners knowledge and skills that would lessen their chances of returning to prison after their release. However, the governor vetoed this bill.

Throughout these endeavors, I relied on the outstanding efforts of my staff. My Sacramento chief of staff, Gail Evans, deftly oversaw a large staff with direction, encouragement, and problem-solving skills. The staff performed myriad tasks that made my job possible. They analyzed the bills on which I had to vote and did research on my own bills. They welcomed visitors, lobbyists, and constituents to my office. My district office in Pasadena met with and answered phone calls from constituents and represented me at many events in my district. Both my capitol and district offices were essential to my success in the senate.

One aspect of my senate years that I particularly enjoyed was the rich ethnic diversity of my senatorial district, which included African

Americans, Asian Americans, Latinos, Armenian Americans, and others. I frequently attended ethnic events in my district. I regularly attended the celebration of Martin Luther King Jr.'s birthday and participated in the Black History parade. I also enjoyed the parade celebrating the Chinese New Year, since I represented a portion of Chinatown. My district included Glendale, which has the largest Armenian American population in the nation (approximately sixty thousand). Lacreta and I attended many events featuring Armenian culture and food. In turn, I was successful in establishing an Armenia/California trade office in Yerevan, the capital of Armenia. Armenian groups sponsored me for two trips to Armenia to bring this to fruition. These interactions in my district and in the legislature led me to a deeper understanding of the different cultures that make up America.

And certainly one of the great benefits of my service in the legislature was the deep friendships I formed with other legislators. Sometimes people ask me what politicians are like. I simply say that they are like people in general. Some are persons of integrity and high ability; some, on the other hand, are not. Some of them shared my political views; some did not. Alan Lowenthal from Long Beach was a legislator of integrity and skill. He and I played racquetball on a weekly basis and discussed issues, spiced with humor, on our game breaks. I learned from the wisdom of John Vasconcellos, who served in the legislature for over thirty years, before the term limits were put in effect. Two outstanding and brilliant women, Sheila Kuehl and Jackie Speier, became treasured friends and colleagues. During my last two years, I shared a desk with a thoughtful and kind man, Darrell Steinberg, who later became senator pro tempore and then mayor of Sacramento.

Other friends were from "across the aisle." Bob Margett, a Republican, represented the district just east of mine. We loved to kid each other about our differing political views. He would call me a "pinko liberal," and I would then refer to him as "Genghis Khan." But we were friends who respected and continued to visit each other after our retirements. I made it a rule never to attack a legislator personally. We could debate vigorously, but I refused to insult anyone. I only wish that some of our present politicians would follow this practice.

I decided to retire from legislative service when my term ended in 2008. I look back on my twelve years (1996–2008) in the California legislature fondly. It was an enjoyable experience, and I believe I served the common good. Creating laws and influencing state politics allowed me to positively impact the lives of thousands of people. In doing so, I was also able to achieve some of Adam's dreams. Certainly, I made some mistakes in practice, but my principles were clear. Once, I was asked what biblical scripture I would use as my guide in public life. I replied that I would attempt to follow the guidance of Micah 6:8: "What does the LORD require of you but to do justice, and to love kindness, and to walk humbly with your God?"

CHAPTER 9

A Time to Retire, A Time to Grieve

(2009–Present)

Figure 9.1. Jack kissing Lacreta, 2019

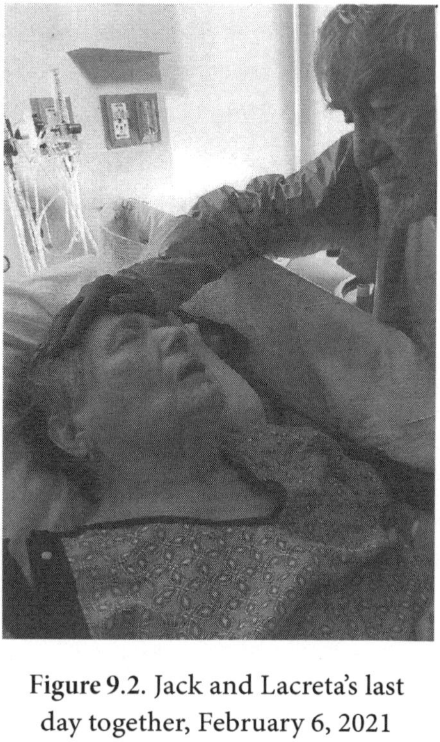

Figure 9.2. Jack and Lacreta's last day together, February 6, 2021

In the fall of 2008, I decided to retire from work at the end of my senate term. I had served the California State Senate limit of eight years, and I did not intend to seek any other public office. I knew the time had come to step back from some of my responsibilities and enjoy my remaining years.

However, there was a vacancy in the position of chancellor of the California Community Colleges (CCC) at this time. My combination of extensive community college administration and legislative experience caused many people to view me as uniquely qualified for the job. A delegation of community college leaders (presidents, faculty, and trustees) came to my office to ask that I apply. Governor Schwarzenegger also sent his chief education aide to express his wish that I seek the position. Becoming chancellor would be an opportunity for me to return to my community college roots.

Lacreta and I discussed this possibility at some length. Since we owned a home in Sacramento and the Office of the Community College Chancellor was in that city, we would not have to move to accept this position. Although I was in good health, I still had to factor in that I was seventy-five years old.

Finally, I informed the Board of Governors of the CCC that I would accept the position if they chose to appoint me. However, I did not want to be one of many candidates. Rather, I suggested that they have a vote on whether to appoint me, and I would be happy with whatever they decided. I appeared before the board of governors for a brief interview, and they unanimously appointed me as chancellor, effective January 1, 2009.

In accepting this job, I fully realized both its possibilities and its limitations. The authority of the CCC chancellor is not absolute; the individual community colleges have elected boards of trustees. These trustees select personnel and approve budgets for their respective colleges. So the chancellor of the CCC does not have the same authority possessed by the heads of the California State University (CSU) and the University of California systems. However, the Chancellor's Office does enforce all statewide laws and regulations pertaining to community colleges.

The chancellor also serves as the chief lobbyist for community colleges, frequently appearing before legislative committees, meeting with individual legislators, and even meeting with the governor on occasion. This does not mean that other community college organizations—such as those representing the interests of faculty, administrators, or trustees—do not also have lobbyists. But the chancellor, as the titular head of the community colleges, is in the unique position of representing the entire system. And if he or she chooses, the chancellor can exercise the "bully pulpit." For instance, an immediate problem that I confronted in 2009 was the national economic recession. As the state budget was reduced, community college funding was substantially cut. Of course, I had earlier lobbied to lessen that impact. But once the budget was settled, I often traveled to colleges to emphasize the importance of their work despite the reduction of funds. And I also suggested where the cuts should be made.

The recession was both a challenge and an opportunity. As many have wisely observed, a crisis is a terrible thing to waste. Colleges now had the opportunity to cut unproductive programs and classes. I recommended that classes designed for transfer and career education be given first priority. Classes of a recreational nature should be considered less important. Since cuts had to be made, those were the classes that should be reduced.

I also determined to initiate some important changes that would improve the overall community college system, which at that time educated over two million students. Two initiatives that were completed during my tenure were particularly important.

The first initiative was the creation of the associate degree for transfer (ADT) between the CCC and CSU. At the time, transfer agreements between community colleges and CSU were done individually through agreements between an individual college and a neighboring CSU. The practice resulted in much confusion. Community college students would often find some of their credits were not transferable to a CSU. Furthermore, one CSU could differ from another as to what was transferable. What was needed was a system-wide transfer system. This could be achieved by four key changes: (1) an agreement on general education requirements between the two systems, (2) an agreement on which community college courses were transferable, (3) the creation by community colleges of a common sixty-unit ADT, and (4) a commitment by CSU that only sixty additional units would be needed to complete a bachelor's degree if a student had an ADT degree. This would save the student a great deal of time and money. It would also save the state money, since the average number of units needed by a transfer student to get a bachelor's degree would generally be reduced.

Fortunately, the chancellor of CSU, Charles Reed, was in favor of this plan. He had come from Florida, which had a similar system that was successful. We were confident that the legislature would favor such a plan, since it was a win for the state and a win for the students. So I went to an effective senator, Alex Padilla, and asked him to carry the bill. There was a groundswell of support for the bill. It easily passed both the assembly and senate and was signed by Governor Schwarzenegger. Once it became law, it required hard work by the academic senates and faculty of the two systems to agree on all the details of this transfer system. It proved to be a resounding success. In the twelve years since the ADT was established, the number of these degrees awarded has increased dramatically:

2012: 749
2013: 5,228
2014: 11,579
2015: 20,760
2016: 31,379
2017: 40,043
2018: 49,850
2019: 58,810
2020: 68,321
2021: 74,145
2022: 70,148
2023: 64,969

Over this twelve-year period, 495,981 community college students in California were awarded the ADT degree. This meant many more students were able to transfer successfully; it also saved these students both time and money. And the savings to the state of California would mean more students could receive a higher education.

The second major initiative of my tenure was the creation of a Student Success Task Force. This addressed a concern intrinsic to the community colleges. On the one hand, community colleges are often praised for their open-door policy (i.e., any high school graduate can be admitted). Because of this policy, millions of students have the opportunity for a college education. In practice, however, too many community college students drop out before reaching their goals. Admittedly, the open-door policy of community colleges naturally leads to more dropouts than in colleges and universities that have a restricted admission policy. The question was, Could community colleges examine their processes and adopt changes that would ensure greater student success—that is, help more students complete their goals?

To address this question, in 2010, I was able to work with Senator Carol Liu to have her author a bill creating a commission that would study and make recommendations to improve student success in CCC. The bill passed and was signed by the governor. Fortunately, funding was provided to support this undertaking. Furthermore, the Board of Governors of the CCC enthusiastically approved this endeavor and empowered me to take the necessary steps to create a Student Success Task Force.

I knew that members of this task force should be knowledgeable and enthusiastic about its purpose. I also recognized that the task force should have broad representation so that our recommendations would have widespread support. The twenty-three members were composed of college presidents, faculty, trustees, researchers, members of the board of governors, and members of the public. I specifically asked Jane Patton, president of the CCC Academic Senate, to participate and to select three other faculty members. I knew that faculty support would be essential to the success of the task force. I also selected Peter MacDougall, a member of the board of governors and a successful former community college president, to chair the task force. Amy Supinger, a consultant and former educational staff person in the state senate, was hired to support the task force by taking minutes, dealing with correspondence, and taking care of all the necessary details.

After the formation of the Student Success Task Force, we began our meetings in Sacramento. We first brought in national experts on student success in community colleges and listened to their testimony. But then the real work began, as we discussed what our own recommendations would be. These were lively discussions, but for the most part, we could reach consensus. On a few occasions when we could not reach consensus, we took a vote to determine a particular recommendation that was favored by the majority. We sought the expertise of individuals outside the task force when we believed we needed additional information. Finally, we drew up a document outlining twenty-two recommendations for student success.

We knew that additional support would be necessary for students to reach their goals, so some of our recommendations dealt with strengthening student services, such as tutoring. We also recommended expanded orientation for entering students. Studies clearly indicated that giving more attention to entering students would guarantee greater success. We required that students declare their educational goals during their first year and choose their major by the second year. In addition, we strongly suggested that remedial education be compressed and reformed. Students should not be required to take two or three semesters of remedial classes before progressing to college coursework. We also instituted a requirement that each college publicize in detail the progress of their students, broken down by ethnicity, to ensure that no groups were disproportionately impacted.

Before finalizing our recommendations, we held three public forums at three community colleges in different areas of the state. We also appeared before groups and solicited written responses. The overall response was positive, but any change in the status quo always incurs opposition. Fortunately, newspaper editorials, business groups, and some educational organizations endorsed our recommendations. On January 9, 2012, the task force presented its recommendations to the board of governors. After a thorough discussion, these recommendations were approved without a dissenting vote. Later that year, we incorporated the recommendations that needed legislative approval in a bill (SB 1456) carried by my friend Senator Alan Lowenthal. The bill passed the senate and assembly and was signed by the governor.

The work of the Student Success Task Force had a lasting impact. Clearly, solid required steps were taken by the board of governors and through legislative action. But equally important, the work of the task force stimulated wide discussion of student success at individual colleges, causing colleges to adopt student success programs tailored to their institution. Another result was that in the next and subsequent budget years, additional funding came to the colleges for student success programs. On occasion, some faculty had argued that what the community colleges needed was more funding for what the colleges were already doing. I responded by stating that we would be more likely to receive increased funding if the community colleges instituted needed reform. Fortunately, my comments proved prophetic.

Meanwhile, I continued my work as chancellor: visiting colleges, lobbying for funding, addressing my support for or opposition to bills before the legislature, and overseeing a staff of about 150 people. Occasionally, I would be called upon to address problems at troubled colleges. For example, I worked with Compton College, which had lost its accreditation but subsequently became a campus of El Camino College. I discussed with them ways in which they might regain their status as an independent college, which was eventually accomplished. I also had to appoint a trustee to oversee San Francisco City College, as they were threatened with the loss of accreditation.

I spent four satisfying and fruitful years as chancellor of the CCC. But in the spring of 2013, I announced my retirement, effective September 1. This decision did not reflect any dissatisfaction with the position. Had I been younger, I would have gladly continued as chancellor. However, at the age of seventy-nine, I believed it was an appropriate time to retire.

Retirement would allow Lacreta and me to move back to Pasadena and pursue other tasks at a more leisurely pace. Furthermore, announcing my retirement early would give the board of governors sufficient time to find a replacement. I had an excellent replacement in mind: Brice Harris, recently retired chancellor of the Los Rios Community College District, which was headquartered in Sacramento. I went to lunch with him, looked him in the eye, and asked him, "Would you be interested in being chancellor?" When he expressed some interest, I knew we had the right person. I encouraged Brice, and the board wisely chose him to succeed me on September 1, 2012.

Returning to our lives in Pasadena, however, was far more complicated than Lacreta and I anticipated. In 2011, our house in Altadena burned down on Christmas Day. We were returning from church that Sunday morning when a police car stopped us as we drove up the street leading to our home. When I asked the officer why we were stopped, he explained that a house was on fire. I told him our address. To our great dismay, he told us that the house that was burning was ours. Despite the firefighters' best efforts, we watched helplessly as our house burned to the ground.

As our home went up in flames, Lacreta philosophically said, "Well, it was just stuff."

And I added, "What I mind most of all will be the hassle."

We had learned perspective the hard way. Our sense of loss for the house was minor compared to losing Adam in 1993. There are losses far more painful than that of material things.

But I was right about the hassle. Fortunately, we had good insurance with State Farm. However, we still had to have the mess cleaned up. We then had to itemize every item that was lost. Finally, we had to construct a new house. I had never wanted to oversee the construction of a new house, but in this case, we had no choice. Lacreta shouldered much of the work in this process, as I was still working full-time as chancellor in Sacramento when the house burned. We greatly improved our house with a new floor plan and even added an upstairs with two bedrooms and a bath. We knew that the added cost of this would be more than repaid when we eventually sold the house.

We lived in a condominium for two years while we waited for our house to be completed. However, as the reconstruction moved toward the end, we reversed course and began to seriously consider downsizing to a smaller home. We contacted a realtor and found exactly what we wanted: a three-bedroom condominium located on one floor on historic Orange Grove Boulevard in Pasadena. We purchased the condominium, sold our reconstructed house at a nice profit, and moved into our new home in December 2013. We continued to enjoy this home for many years and were happy with our decision.

Though the term *retirement* implies leisurely inactivity, my retirement has been characterized by meaningful endeavors. Shortly after the announcement of my retirement, I received a letter from Scott Thomas, dean of the School of Education at Claremont Graduate University. I had kept a connection with the university in the years since completing my doctorate, including being named their Distinguished Alumnus in 2000. Scott wrote that he would like to meet with me and discuss ways in which I might be helpful to the university. We met and explored this possibility. The university offered to designate me as a Scholar in Residence. In this role, I would deliver a key lecture, advise them on community college issues, and teach or coteach some graduate classes. This proved to be a great opportunity for me to deliver lectures, teach, and conduct workshops, and Scott and I became close friends.

I also have kept busy in other ways. For several years, I served as a consultant to the Los Angeles Chamber of Commerce on ways in which the business world and education could work together. For three years, I attended their national conferences and participated in panels on this subject. I also consulted with Bakersfield College, Cerritos College, and Mount San Antonio College to improve the fundraising capabilities of their foundations. In 2015, I was asked to return to Pasadena City College (PCC) and serve on their foundation board. They put me to work rather quickly by asking me to head up a fundraising campaign in 2016. During this two-year campaign, we were able to raise $16 million, thus exceeding our goal of $10 million. I currently serve on two statewide boards: California Competes and the Higher Education Advisory Council of the Public Policy Institute of California. These organizations are designed to make recommendations to improve higher education in California.

This list of endeavors sounds like I am constantly busy. The reality is that the time required is not nearly as much as when I was working full-time. I enjoy making a contribution where I have some expertise, but I also enjoy having more free time.

By 2013, Lacreta had also retired. Our retirements enabled us to have precious time to spend together and to travel. One of our most memorable trips was a safari to Kenya and Tanzania with our good friends Jim Kossler and Margie Lewis. Each day, a guide took the four of us to see animals in the wild. We saw hundreds of animals in their natural habitat, including lions, elephants, giraffes, crocodiles, zebras, and cheetahs. For instance, one day at dusk, a female leopard crossed in front of our vehicle, making a barking sound. Suddenly, her two cubs appeared, and she began leading them to a kill.

We also took three cruises during this time. In 2015, we had just returned from a Baltic cruise when we received the news that our daughter-in-law, Paula, was seriously ill. She had suffered a cardiac arrest. We rushed to be with her and Greg in Texas, where we stayed with my sister and brother-in-law, Patsy and Foy Vinson. Paula was in a coma for several days, but fortunately, she fully recovered.

While we were in Texas, though, Lacreta developed a fever and was diagnosed with pneumonia. She received a prescription from an urgent care facility. When she did not fully recover soon, we assumed it was a reaction to the prescription. However, Lacreta's health problems worsened after we returned to Pasadena. We consulted with our primary physician, Dr. Todd Turner. He tentatively diagnosed her with an autoimmune disease, polymyalgia rheumatica, and referred her to a specialist. After several visits with a rheumatologist, this specialist finally determined that she did not have this disease, but the rheumatologist was unable to make a definite diagnosis. Soon Lacreta began to have some difficulty with walking. First, she used a cane, but eventually, she needed a walker. At this point, Dr. Turner thought the problem might be Parkinson's disease, so he referred Lacreta to a neurologist, Dr. Tyler Cheung.

Dr. Cheung ran a test and quickly determined that Lacreta was suffering from hydrocephalus, a condition affecting senior citizens where spinal fluid does not drain well from the brain. The resulting pressure can cause difficulties in walking, talking, and urinary incontinence. So in June 2018, Dr. William Caton, a neurosurgeon, installed a shunt in Lacreta's brain. Although this resulted in some improvement, Dr. Cheung began to suspect there was a more serious condition underlying the hydrocephalus. On August 22, 2018, he diagnosed Lacreta with progressive supranuclear palsy (PSP). PSP is a rare, incurable brain disease; there are only 160,000 cases reported in the United States. It does not affect cognition. However, Lacreta's speech was badly affected; she could only say a few words. She often did not feel well. Finally, she was reduced to having to use a wheelchair.

All this caused many changes in our daily life. We hired two caregivers. They alternated so that one would be with her from eight to six o'clock each day. I would take care of Lacreta in the evening. I took over many responsibilities, including grocery shopping, taking her to doctors, going to drugstores, and so forth. I found caring for her to be a privilege; after all, she had given me such loving care through the years.

The changes in her were painful to see. I was deeply touched as I watched her struggles. She was very brave, but for someone who was so verbal and intelligent, it was extremely hard for her not to be able to talk. A skilled conversationalist and writer who loved words, she had been silenced by this cruel disease. I constantly told her how much I loved her and what she had meant in my life. She had been everything to me for over sixty years. Interestingly, though she could no longer speak, she could sometimes join me in singing a song or a hymn. On one occasion, she indicated to me that she wanted a pen and a piece of paper. With some difficulty, she wrote, "I love you." I was deeply touched.

On January 31, 2021, Lacreta began to cough a great deal. I was worried and had her taken to the hospital. The next morning, the hospital called me and said she was suffering from COVID-19. We don't know how Lacreta contracted the disease. She and I had received our first vaccination shots ten days earlier. But Lacreta was in a weakened condition because of her disease, and we know that senior citizens are more vulnerable to the virus.

Because of the pandemic, I wasn't able to visit her in the hospital. However, for the next few days, the doctors informed me that she was doing well, and I was hopeful. But she took a turn for the worse on Thursday, and on Saturday, February 6, they told me she could not survive.

The hospital graciously permitted me to be with her that final morning. They allowed our daughter Sheila to join me. Lacreta was on a breathing machine, but she was conscious. We told her how much we loved her and sang some hymns.

As we held her hands, Sheila asked her, "Mom, are you ready to go?"

Lacreta squeezed our hands. She obviously knew she was dying, and she was ready. My beloved wife, Lacreta Isbell Scott, passed away at 2:45 p.m. on February 6, 2021.

My only consolation about Lacreta dying from the virus was that she was already destined to die from PSP and was obviously getting weaker and weaker. But I miss her more than words can express. I feel like half of me is gone. But I have great consolation as I recall the wonderful memories of our life together.

We were a team. I always treasured her wisdom and unselfish nature as we worked together. As we considered dramatic moves, she would give her insights and be encouraging and supportive. This was true of our move to New Haven, our cross-country transition to Pepperdine, and my entrance into political life.

We had great joy in our travels. She relished the sights we saw and made light of the difficulties we experienced. I can still picture Lacreta on our bicycle trips. She would climb hills with gusto and fill our time with laughter.

The highlight of my day was to come home after work and sit down to the delicious dinner that Lacreta had cooked. We would then share our day. For instance, she might tell me about her teaching at Cerritos College, and I might tell her about the problems I solved or needed to solve at PCC.

After Lacreta's death, I received many cards and letters describing how Lacreta had impacted the writers' lives. One such letter was from Emma Whitson, a graduate student in English at CSU, Long Beach. She is the daughter of Beverly Whitson, Lacreta's office mate at Cerritos College. Emma told me that in class one day, her professor, Dr. Amaris, had told everyone about a teacher at Cerritos College named "Lacreta" who had changed her life.

Emma went up after class and asked Dr. Amaris if she was referring to Lacreta Scott. Dr. Amaris burst into tears. She described how Lacreta had encouraged her during one of the most difficult times of her life. At the time, Dr. Amaris had two children and was facing divorce. But Lacreta saw her potential and told her how to fulfill that potential. Dr. Amaris described Lacreta as a wonderful woman who had a huge impact on her life.

Lacreta was buried at Mountain View Cemetery in Altadena on February 20, 2021, next to our son Adam. We could not have a regular memorial service because of the pandemic, but family members were allowed to attend a graveside service. Her brother Allen Isbell presided. In touching words, he described how Lacreta had been present from his first day of life and had influenced him both in his childhood and up to the present. He told a humorous story about being excited when his elementary schoolteacher told him he did not have to do everything his older sister, Lacreta, told him. Upon returning home, he repeated this information to Lacreta. However, he commented that his newfound freedom did not last long as he once again followed Lacreta's direction. Then several of our children and grandchildren shared their wonderful memories. Our daughter Sheila shared a poem she had written about Lacreta, comparing her mother to a fallen tree that continues to nurture the forest in death. Our granddaughter Nicole Rodger described how Lacreta always bought all the granddaughters a special Christmas dress. The shopping trips inevitably included new shoes and accessories and often ended with Lacreta advising the girls, "We don't need to tell your grandfather how much all this cost." The service was a true celebration of life, filled with a tangible sense of the loving presence Lacreta was throughout our lives. We all realized that we had been privileged to live with such an amazing person.

Losing Lacreta was one of the hardest things I have ever experienced. But I would be ungrateful if I filled my life with self-pity rather than thanksgiving. I was blessed beyond measure to meet and marry such a person, and I am still grateful for her every day.

EPILOGUE

A Time to Reflect

Figure 10.1. Family attending the Jack Scott Administration Building dedication

Figure 10.2. Jack Scott Administration Building, Pasadena City College, 2021

On August 24, 2023, I celebrated my ninetieth birthday. I know not what the future holds, but whether I live one more year or ten more years, it is clear that I am in the last stage of my life. So I now will close this memoir with a few reflections.

Since Lacreta's death, I have continued to stay busy. I realized that it would not be productive for me to become reclusive and bury myself in grief. For instance, I counsel drug addicts and alcoholics at the Salvation Army on Tuesday and Thursday afternoons. I volunteered to assist this Christian organization, and they believed that I could be particularly helpful as a spiritual counselor. I began this work on September 1, 2020, and continued it after Lacreta's passing. These men are in a six-month program of rehabilitation. I compliment them for seeking help, listen to their stories, emphasize that God loves and forgives them, and occasionally offer advice.

Six months after Lacreta's death, our family experienced another sorrow. Rick Head, our daughter Sheila's husband, died on August 1, 2021. Rick's death was expected, since he was suffering from terminal cancer. He had bravely fought this battle for several years. His funeral was held at the North Oaks Church of Christ. A large crowd was present. I was able to visit in their home often prior to Rick's passing. Sheila and I continue to comfort each other in our widowed condition.

On November 21, 2021, I received a wonderful surprise. Bobbi Abram, from the Pasadena City College Foundation Board, asked me to attend the meeting of the board of trustees. She stated that she wanted me to support her in a report she was going to present. Suddenly, at the beginning of the meeting, I was called to the podium. Then it was announced that the board of trustees had unanimously decided to name the PCC Administration Building in my honor. I was overwhelmed. It is a beautiful building facing Colorado Boulevard, overlooking the reflection pools of the college, where a small plaque in Adam's honor is placed. I can now drive by the college and see my name inscribed on this wonderful building.

As for my present status, I am in excellent health for a person of my age. No doubt, some of this is due to a fortunate genetic inheritance. I have also exercised regularly for all my life and have been wise enough to seek medical assistance when needed. For instance, I always get an annual physical. I am aware that the body declines. Nevertheless, I believe that we are called upon to serve as long as we are privileged to live.

I am also fortunate to be financially secure. I never took a job based on compensation, but in the latter half of my life, I was paid well. So with retirement income, Social Security, and investments, I feel blessed. I often humorously say, "I will run out of time before I run out of money."

I have been blessed beyond measure throughout my life, and I am profoundly grateful. First, I thank God for these rich gifts. These blessings did not come my way because I deserved them. As Paul accurately stated, "For by grace you have been saved through faith; and this is not your own doing, it is the gift of God" (Eph. 2:8). And I am confident of God's grace. I am not arrogant enough to think I can exactly identify all that God has done. Yet as I review my life and recall the doors that were suddenly opened for me, I cannot help but thank God for his guidance. And as I review my sins and mistakes, I am very grateful that God has forgiven me.

I owe a great deal to many, many people. In no way would I claim to be a self-made man. From the beginning, I was blessed with loving, nurturing parents. I have a picture in my office of myself at one year of age. My hair is perfectly combed. I am holding a large ball, and I have a contented look on my face. I know it was the loving hand of my mother that made that picture possible. Furthermore, I was given a set of moral and religious values by my parents that served me well throughout my life.

And who can calculate the powerful impact of friends? I will not attempt to list all these important friends; I mentioned some of them earlier in this memoir. But beginning in elementary school and up to the present time, friends have been very important to me. They have provided countless hours of humor and laughter, but they have also provided me with many hours of serious discussion. At times they have changed my mind or certainly improved my thinking on many topics. Since Lacreta's passing, I have been blessed by the friendship of Francine Dabao, who began as Lacreta's caregiver and became a dear friend to us both. She provides assistance to me in the practical needs of my life, such as cleaning and cooking. In the Tennessee Williams classic *A Streetcar Named Desire*, Blanche DuBois utters the famous line "I have always depended on the kindness of strangers." I would like to amend this slightly. I have always depended on the kindness of friends.

Yes, teachers have been very important to me. I still remember some dedicated teachers in the public schools in Sweetwater. But it was the professors in higher education at Abilene Christian University, Yale Divinity School, and Claremont Graduate University who changed my life. One reason I spent most of my career in colleges was that I realized from my own experience that college was a place where I could make a profound difference.

My own family has been supremely important. My children blessed me: Sharon, Sheila, Amy, Greg, and Adam. No one does parenting perfectly; I can compile a long list of my failures. But it was a wonderful, enriching experience to interact with my children, and it continues to this day. I once remarked to Lacreta that we were so blessed that all our children were good people. This was far more important to us than their success in other ways. But I must admit that no one influenced me as deeply as Lacreta did. I have already filled this memoir with praising her. She made an immeasurable impact on my life.

My religious beliefs continue to be the core of my life, but over the years, they have grown and matured with experience. As a youth, I was steeped in Churches of Christ. It was all I knew. However, I began to discover that despite its strengths, this fellowship, like all human institutions, is not infallible. I could no longer believe we were "the only true church." I did not choose to divorce myself from Churches of Christ, but

I did discover rich spiritual truths by reading from authors outside the Church of Christ and frequent attendance at other churches.

Fortunately, I have seen some changes occurring. Some congregations are no longer patriarchal; women are leading prayer and even preaching. Both the Abilene Christian and Pepperdine lectureships have had women preaching. These groups are also listening occasionally to ministers from other churches. Some Churches of Christ are no longer featuring repeated sermons on what is wrong with other churches. Of course, I am sure there are those in Churches of Christ who consider all these recent changes as rank heresy, but I believe the changes are healthy.

Every year I attend the Christian Scholars Conference, generally held at Lipscomb University. Here controversial subjects are freely discussed, speakers outside Churches of Christ are featured, and people can disagree without denouncing one another as unscriptural or heretical. It is refreshing to see old friends there and to find an atmosphere of freedom.

I am fully aware that I don't possess absolute truth religiously. Paul himself stated that we only "know in part" and that "we see in a mirror dimly" (1 Cor. 13:12). I always want to be open to a better understanding, to be willing to seek the truth wherever it leads me. I am confident that God's grace in the last day will forgive our lack of understanding, just as he graciously forgives our sins.

In closing, I thank those of you who have continued to read this memoir. I hope it has been helpful to you, the reader. As I stated in my introduction, it has certainly been meaningful for me to retrace the journey of my life. And I want to conclude with Paul's words, which I hope capture my present thought in both affirming life and facing inevitable death: "For I am sure that neither death, nor life, nor angels, nor principalities, nor things present, nor things to come, nor powers, nor height, nor depth, nor anything else in all creation, will be able to separate us from the love of God in Christ Jesus our Lord" (Rom. 8:38–39).

Figure 10.3. In loving memory, 1954

ACKNOWLEDGMENTS

So many people have greatly enriched my life (my parents, teachers, friends, my children, and Lacreta) that it would not be possible to acknowledge them all. However, throughout this memoir, I have made it clear that many people have made immeasurable contributions to my life. Unfortunately, Lacreta, an accomplished writer and former English teacher, could not contribute directly to this project. She passed away shortly after I began this memoir. The memoir is, however, dedicated to her.

But I do want to acknowledge those who specifically contributed to the writing of this memoir. After the first draft, I asked certain friends to review it: Zane Reeves, David Fleer, Greg Sterling, Jim Wilburn, Richard Hughes, and my daughter Sheila Scott Head. They all gave me excellent and helpful suggestions that improved this memoir.

At that stage, though, it dawned on me that I had a friend who was an accomplished ghostwriter, Mary Jane Ross. An editor and former English professor, she had ghostwritten seven memoirs, all of which had sold well. I talked with her about my project, and she agreed to help me. She proceeded to edit my writing, including suggestions for sentence revision and rearranging of paragraphs. Her insights about the possible publication of this memoir were great. Her many suggestions were very helpful; she assisted me immeasurably in the final product of this memoir.

For the help of these friends, I am truly grateful.